"What are you doing here, young lady?"

Ahh!
This is the greatest mistake I've made in my life!

"Mommy told me not to talk to strangers..."

Mitsuha used her signature move: Act Like a Child!

"Ogres! A whole pack of them!"

Ogres were the strongest monsters that inhabited the area. And out of nowhere, there was a horde practically right on top of them.

"U-Um, Rudina... How old are you?"

"I'm thirteen!"

"Why did you apply to this café?"

"Because there was no age requirement on the application!"

Oh, I forgot to add that...

Saving 80,000 Gold in Another World for My Retirement

for My Retirement

Story by **FUNA**

Art by **Touzai**

4

KODANSHA

Saving 80,000 Gold in Another World for My Retirement 4

A VERTICAL Book

Translation: Luke Hutton
Editor: Momo Fukazawa
Production: Grace Lu
Proofreading: Kevin Luo

Publication rights for this English edition arranged through Kodansha, Ltd., Tokyo. English language version produced by Kodansha USA Publishing, LLC, 2023.

Originally published in Japan as *Rougo ni Sonaete Isekai de 8-Man-Mai no Kinka o Tamemasu 5* by Kodansha, Tokyo, 2019.

ISBN 978-1-64729-313-0

Printed in the United States of America

First Edition

Kodansha USA Publishing, LLC
451 Park Avenue South, 7th Floor
New York, NY 10016
www.kodansha.us

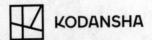 KODANSHA

CONTENTS

DESIGN: Yuko Mukadeya + Hideyuki Uekusa (Musicago Graphics)

Chapter 39:
The Return of the Archpriestess

Mitsuha decided it was time to go home with Sabine and Colette. She certainly was *not* shirking her duty, and she wouldn't hear any complaints suggesting as much.

The three of them left Coursos once they finished their duty of demonstrating the new weapon. After they departed the city on foot, Mitsuha summoned the *Lollipop* with her world-jumping powers without being seen. Count Kolbmane was *not* happy that the girls left the rest of the delegation tasks to him, and he let Mitsuha hear it over the radio.

The remainder of the journey had its ups and downs, including some hiccups in the country after Coursos, but the delegation ended up successfully visiting all of the planned stops, and were finally ready to head back home.

It ended up taking about two and a half months to visit every country, Mitsuha thought. *Most of the negotiations went smoothly. We did run into some trouble, but it wasn't too different from what we experienced in the first two countries. Nothing worth recounting.*

Because the delegation could report their progress in real time over wireless radio, the king didn't have to wait for Count Kolbmane's delegates to return before sending the main delegation that would perform the official treaty conference. Princess Remia from Dalisson and the king from Coursos had already signed the treaty. *Nice to see that people can learn and improve.*

And so, after the delegation finished talks with the farthest country on their agenda, they began the journey home.

Mitsuha collected the *Lollipop*, which she had hidden outside the capital of the final country, and then said goodbye to Count Kolbmane and the others.

"We're gonna get going. See you at the royal palace!"

"Huh?" Count Kolbmane and Clarge both looked puzzled.

"We've already finished our mission, so there's no reason for us to meet up again. The girls and I are going right back to the capital. The next time we'll see you will be at the palace—you know, when they throw a celebratory event for your triumphant return…"

"What?! No!"

The delegation was returning to Zegleus on the same route they came. The plan was to meet with each country's leaders again and inform them of how the pre-treaty talks went with the others. A second welcome party upon their arrival was well expected at each site.

No thank you! They don't need us for that!

These last two and a half months felt like an eternity to Mitsuha. Even jumping back to her home base on occasion didn't help. She definitely couldn't go back to the capital though. She wasn't about to demonstrate how freely she could use her world-jumping ability.

I've had my fill of international travel. Taking a different route back might've made it bearable, but there's no way in hell I could handle going through the same exact countries again. I'd rather just jump home. Sabine and Colette feel the same.

"P-P-Please wait! What will we say when we arrive at the welcome parties without the star of the sho—"

"Bye! Safe travels!"

The girls, ignoring the count's desperate attempts to stop them, climbed into the *Lollipop* and floored the accelerator.

Leaving like this might inconvenience the rest of the delegation, but another round of attending parties and having nobles compete over me with endless solicitations? Count me out! Too-da-loo!

Mitsuha jumped to her house in Japan. They needed to kill some time. There would've been no explanation for how they arrived in the capital so quickly after leaving the delegation.

… That's why we're taking a weeklong vacation. We don't have much time left today, so we're just gonna go to the usual department store and smack down some kids' meals.

"M-Mitsuha, are you done yet?"

"Don't rush me, Colette!"

"Why did you go first, Mitsuha?!" whined Sabine. "You should've jumped us to a different bathroom before you took the only open stall! What were you thinking?!"

"S-Sorry…"

So much for learning and improving…

The second day.

"We're going to an amusement park today!" Mitsuha announced.

"What's that?"

"You'll see! I'm taking you to the best one in Japan!"

Amusement parks apparently hadn't come up in any of the anime Sabine and Colette had watched.

"AAAHHH!" screamed all three girls.

"Why are you screaming too, Mitsuha?!"

"This is actually the first time I've been to this one!"

Roller coasters are something else!

Oh, we got here by world-jumping, of course. I don't wanna waste time or money on travel!

The third day.

"Today, we're going to Tokyu Hands!"

We spent the entire day exploring the massive DIY craft store, only stopping for food and bathroom breaks, and still didn't get to see every floor... Tokyu Hands is something else!

The fourth day.

"We're going to Mount Fuji today!"

Yeah, you heard me. We're going to Mount Fuji, not hiking it. By jumping, of course. Admiring Mount Fuji from the bottom is way better than climbing it, especially in the evening. There's a fantastic, otherworldly beauty to Mount Fuji. It's the tallest mountain in Japan but that's not what it's celebrated for. That magnetism you experience when you're gazing up at it—you can't help but feel that it's worthy of its title as a sacred mountain.

Sabine and Colette, who had heard of Mount Fuji from anime, looked at it with wonder and awe.

We went to the summit too. By jumping, of course.

"Mitsuha, this doesn't feel rewarding at all!" Sabine complained.

"Yeah, you ruined it!" Colette followed.

...I guess I should've expected that response.

Mitsuha and the girls went to a few more fun places on the fifth and sixth days. Finally came the seventh day.

"Hellooo! Can I have this one, sir?" Mitsuha called out.

"Well, if it isn't Ms. Yamano!"

They arrived at the Solar Ray shop. By now, Mitsuha had become a regular customer.

Whoops, solar energy, not Solar Ray. I'm not about to attack a space fortress. I'm here because of a promise I made. Gotta keep your promises, except for the ones you're forced into.

"Can I please have the same set as last time?"

"Yes ma'am! I'll prepare it right away!" the employee answered.

This was Mitsuha's fourth time at the solar energy store, which sped up the process quite a lot. The third set she purchased was the one she installed in Sabine's room in the royal palace. It was battery operated, and produced just enough power to run the bare essentials like a wireless radio, an LED stand, and a small electric fan. Mitsuha had given Sabine a small refrigerator instead of a fan. But for Remia, a fan would be more than enough to call a bonus.

Mitsuha arranged for the solar panel system to be delivered to her house and headed home. She'd bought four sets in a short period of time, and two of them were quite big. The store probably considered her one of their valued customers by now. They gave her a discount and even threw in some freebies. This time, they knew better than to offer an installation service, as Mitsuha had refused the first three times.

I wonder what they think of me... That I have vacation homes across Japan and my hobby is setting up solar panels in them? I've become a pro at this; I could get a part-time job at their store installing the systems if I ever need a little cash.

"Princess Remia, we're here!"

"Oh, M-Mitsy!"

Wait, when did she start calling me that? It feels a little awkward having her refer to me with such a cutesy nickname since I'm older than her. I doubt she'd believe me if I told her she's younger than me, though... Whatever, I'm used to this!

"You always show up with no warning..." Remia sighed.

I hear that all the time from the captain!

"I brought the goods as I promised." Mitsuha and the girls unloaded the parts they were carrying for the solar energy system. It'd be suspicious if Mitsuha arrived empty-handed when they were going to install it—suspicious to everyone except Remia, that is.

Won't Princess Remia be suspicious too, you ask? Ahaha...

Mitsuha, Sabine, and Colette couldn't carry all the equipment at once, so they only brought a portion of it. Mitsuha was going to jump the rest directly into Remia's room.

"All right, time to start!" Mitsuha declared.

"Okay!" Sabine and Colette chimed. They were here as assistants.

Mitsuha made a promise to Remia on the day of the pre-treaty talks that she'd help her if she ever ended up in trouble. She could only keep this promise if Remia had a way to contact her in the event of a crisis. *You know, like a radio, a radio, or maybe even a radio. Hence the solar energy system.*

The installation wasn't too difficult this time. It's not like they were placing tiles on the roof. Remia summoned a team of hand-workers to help, so all Mitsuha had to do was sneak in the rest of the parts, give simple orders, and fiddle with the wiring. They were finished in no time.

Mitsuha already gave away her traversal secret when she arrived at the palace just hours after the delegation was attacked by bandits. She wasn't worried about hiding it around Remia and the hand-

The Return of the Archpriestess

workers, but she made sure to swear them to silence.

Sabine taught Remia how to play reversi and shogi over the radio. You could play by saying "white to 2D" and "silver to 5G" and so on.

If you keep using the radio to play games, you'll kill the battery and won't be able to call for help when you need it...

Mitsuha explained to Remia how to operate the radio, and the princess seemed to grasp everything immediately. Her Highness sure was smart. She didn't just memorize the order in which she had to push the buttons; she actually demonstrated an understanding of what each one did. Unless it broke completely, she'd be able to fix the radio herself if she ever hit the wrong button.

Mitsuha and Remia agreed that the princess would call her once every three days, and that if Mitsuha didn't get a call for twenty-four hours without prior notice, it was assumed that there was an emergency. Mitsuha initially suggested the calls to be once a week, but Remia argued that "a week is too long, make it three days..." so three days it was.

...I'm on to you, Princess Remia, Mitsuha thought. *Safety procedure isn't the only reason you want to make the calls. Talking to her every three days sounds like a pain, so I'm gonna delegate this task to Sabine! Mwahaha!*

"Mitsuha, I expect compensation for this," bartered Sabine.

Oh, come on...

On the way out after installing the solar panel system, Remia stopped the girls.

She said, "We've decided to throw a welcome party/reversi tournament for the three of you tonight. There are prizes involved. The court ladies and maids are on edge. They'll be furious if I cancel it now..."

15

Aw man... We're stuck here, aren't we...

Mitsuha and the girls didn't escape until evening the next day. They had a reservation at a French restaurant waiting for them. The full-course meal was 12,800 yen per person—Sabine and Colette wouldn't miss that for the world.

Remia made a display of chewing on a handkerchief in frustration as the trio hastily departed.

"We're back!" Sabine announced.

The three girls had walked from the capital's gate to the palace, straight to the king's study.

On the way, the gate guards, as well as the palace guards, were dumbfounded by the girls' presence.

"S-Sabine?! H-How did you... Where is Viscountess Yamano? What happened to the delegation?" the king stammered as Sabine walked in.

"Oh, we're with her," Mitsuha chimed in as she and Colette rushed into the room after Sabine.

"Viscountess Yamano! Where are Count Kolbmane and the rest of the delegation?!"

"We decided to leave early without them. The journey would've taken forever if we stayed with the delegation..."

"Ah... Right, you have something called a 'Lolly-pop,' which you charged me as a necessary expense..."

"Er, haha, yeah..."

The Lollipop was really expensive, so I charged him for it in addition to my fee for going on the journey. I bought it on Earth. Which meant that with the exchange rate, it cost a fortune in this world's money. I had to tell him a little about the Lollipop for that reason. He couldn't refuse to pay for it once I told him it would be important for

Sabine's safety and living situation.

"So you snubbed all the welcome parties that were meant for the delegation's return trip… I'm sure all those who regretted taking you lightly the first time around are waiting with bated breath for another chance to get on your good side…" the king agonized.

"That's why I bulldozed my way through!"

The king smiled awkwardly as if to show he understood as much.

Wait a second. Why is the king surprised to see us? Has Count Kolbmane not given him any reports?

There was little need to report now that the delegation's mission was over. They were unlikely to be attacked, and if anything did happen, the count would use the radio to ask for help. There was always someone waiting by the radio in the royal palace—Sabine's room, to be more precise. He'd have plenty of time to ask for help after spotting the raiders. It's not like there's any chance of getting attacked by a rocket launcher in this world.

Which means… They haven't sent a report because they're hoping to meet us in a town. They might be expecting us to sightsee for a few days along the road home and catch up eventually. Is that why they didn't tell the king we left them behind?

Sorry, guys. We're already back.

"Your Majesty, please tell them we've arrived at the capital the next time they call," I requested.

I'd feel awful if they're traveling as fast as they could on the false hope of catching up to us… I'd feel awful for the horses, that is.

Oh, speaking of horses. I need to go check on Silver.

Mitsuha had entrusted the stable to pass her horse along to a farm. Given the length of her absence, it was better than leaving him at the orphanage. Silver probably missed her.

As for the carriage, she left that to the orphanage's care. It was

probably squeaky clean from being polished every day. Hopefully they didn't polish it too much; she didn't want them wearing through the paint.

All right. I'm feeling lazy, so I'll let Sabine handle reporting to the king. I already told him about the important stuff over the radio. Besides, Sabine probably needs some quality time with her parents and siblings. No matter how much energy she has, she's still just a ten-year-old.

After Mitsuha left the palace, she jumped with Colette to her village. She determined the girl needed an extended break after the long journey. Colette had just turned nine, so she was even younger than Sabine.

"Dad! Mom!" she called out excitedly.

"Colette!" her parents cried.

I may as well go visit the Bozeses while I'm at it…

She popped by her county to take care of a few matters, and then jumped to the capital to open Mitsuha's General Store for the first time in a while. She jotted down a to-do list as she tended the store.

I've been putting off some of these tasks for so long they're starting to ferment. Wait much longer and I'll have enough fully brewed bottles of stress to fill a pantry.

The first thing on the list was a very important matter that could threaten her livelihood in Japan if she wasn't careful.

"I'd like to submit this form… This is my first time, so I don't really know what I'm doing."

"Ah, yes," the old lady said. "I'll call the person in charge. Please wait over there."

Mitsuha was at the reception desk of her town's tax office. She had just submitted a registration form for new businesses. She used a good deal of her parents' money as an initial investment to establish herself in the other world, and she paid the Wolf Fang mercenaries in Japanese yen before switching to gold. She wanted to convert some of the dollars in her international bank account to yen and transfer them to her Japanese bank account to restore it to its original balance, but that could get her into a lot of trouble if she wasn't careful.

That's right—the matter at hand is taxes. And here I am in the scariest place on Earth: the tax office. I need to make it look like I'm making a living as a Japanese citizen.

Shortly after, the old lady at reception desk called out, "Number sixteen, please come forward!" That was the number on Mitsuha's ticket.

"Hello. My name is Mitsuha Yamano. It's nice to meet you."

The bespectacled man across from her, who was probably around forty years old, looked confounded.

I know, I know. I look young for my age.

"I'm eighteen years old and have graduated high school," she continued. "I'm also the head of my household and just started a sole proprietorship."

"O-Oh, my apologies. Please follow me." Looking embarrassed that he thought the visitor was a child—and that she realized what he was thinking—he led her to a consultation area with plenty of seating. The seats were divided by partitions.

"Here's my form…" Mitsuha handed the man a sheet of paper. She had printed out the form from the website and filled it out by hand. It only asked for simple information including your name, address, and company name. Filling it out took less than a minute. Apparently, handing in this sheet of paper was all it took to start a business.

Talk about easy! Well, submitting documents to pay taxes and becoming a business owner are two different things.

"Let's see... Your trade title is a sculptor. And the name of your company is Colette's Sculptures. Do you want to submit a white or blue tax return form?"

"Oh, blue please. I don't really understand all that stuff, so I'm going to have a tax consultant handle it."

"That's reassuring. I don't see any problems, so I'll go ahead and process this form. Please wait while I make a copy to give you," he said as he stood up.

That took less than thirty seconds! I got all stressed out for nothing! I thought he would be scary and grill me with a bunch of questions, but he was polite and kind.

I guess they're only strict with people who evade taxes and are kind toward everyone else. That makes sense...

And thus, Mitsuha became the owner of a small business in just thirty seconds.

Why the company name? Because using my real name would've been bad for information security. I went with Colette over Sabine because I think it's a cuter name. I would never say that out loud, though.

...Sabine might actually hurt me if she finds out why I chose Colette's name over hers.

Do I have any talent as a sculptor to run a business selling my creations? Of course not. I'm gonna use my secret weapon: world-jumping! I'll sell sculptures from the other world or jump my original creations directly out of the stone blocks.

Workmanship and artistic quality aren't going to matter...because my customers will be me!—under one of my other identities who have citizenship in other countries.

The first thing Mitsuha did after officially becoming a business owner was go right to a tax consulting firm. She made an appointment after thoroughly comparing the websites of multiple tax consultants and picking one that seemed upright. She'd only have herself to blame if the person turned out to be untrustworthy.

The tax consultant explained everything Mitsuha needed to know, and she signed the contract. That freed her from having to worry about filing taxes.

All that was left to do was to return home and make a website for Colette's Sculptures. She wrote all the text in English. She was careful to make it difficult to find on search engines and hard to navigate. She didn't want anyone stumbling upon it and ordering something. She especially didn't want any orders from Japan, so there was no Japanese text on the website.

Mitsuha only made the site as a way to complete her alibi that she was selling sculptures. There would be no way to explain how an eighteen-year-old girl was selling art overseas with no connections or publicity otherwise. As long as she posted an ad in English, she could claim that some overseas connoisseurs found it, went to the website, and bought her sculptures.

It's perfect!

Lastly, it was time to make some sculptures. She couldn't get away with having no sample pictures on the website. It'd be too suspicious for a website selling art to have zero photos of said art.

She jumped to an unclaimed rocky mountain, rich in natural limestones. There was no property owner who'd get mad at her for cutting a slice or two. She plucked out some blocks from the mountain and jumped it back to her house in Japan while cutting out a shape. She then jumped high above the mountain to drop the excess stone—evidence destroyed. Disposing of the hollow remainders of the stones this way was cumbersome, but she didn't want anyone to find them and make a fuss.

Mitsuha returned to her house and inspected the sculpture she carved out of the stone. It was…not bad. She attempted to mimic a famous sculptor using this technique once before, and the results were disastrous. It was obvious she had no artistic talent. She decided she would outsource all her more traditional sculptures. Her works would be in the "abstract" category.

The first one she made out of the stone was a seamless chain link. Next, she made a stone sphere with a fishnet pattern and placed a deformed animal figure inside. She made another fishnet-patterned sphere and placed some store-bought expensive crystal glass inside. One after another, she created pieces that would either confuse people as to how they were made or look like they took absolutely forever to carve.

She continued to work until she built up a decent stock of sculptures. *These will do.*

Mitsuha spent the next day going to different shops in the capital. At each one, she asked the same question:

"Do you have any sculptures made by up-and-coming artists with potential? And small enough that I can carry home?"

She was looking for sculptures to buy and resell as part of her Colette's Sculptures business; she had no sculpting talent herself, so this was a necessity.

There was a reason she asked for sculptures made by new artists. Her status as a viscountess meant people would default to trying to sell her stupidly expensive sculptures made by renowned artists. It'd be cheaper to buy sculptures that looked like they were made by rookies with potential, and she would also be supporting struggling young artists. That would save her some money and help artists who weren't yet able to make a living. *Everyone wins!*

But the employees and shop owners just wouldn't get the message.

"I recommend this sculpture of a naked lady by Aylarith!"

"This here is the family heirloom of a viscount…"

"No," Mitsuha shook her head. "I said I want something made by a budding artist! I won't buy anything from a famous sculptor. No family heirlooms either. I just want works of decent quality made by artists that no one has ever heard of."

The employees refused to listen no matter how many times she emphasized that, insisting that only their most expensive works were worthy of furnishing her estate. She was at a loss.

I wonder if they sell to all customers this way, or if they're only doing this because I'm a noble. It's hard being famous…

Mitsuha fled the pushy shop on the main street and walked into a back alley for a breather. There, she spotted a cozy little art shop—the kind that was likely managed by the owner alone. Thinking that a smaller art store like this was less likely to be so obnoxious, she went inside. The owner didn't rush toward her. She leisurely inspected the items on the display shelves.

Hey, these are pretty good! Mitsuha thought upon finding a collection of wooden and stone sculptures. The wooden sculptures were a little roughly hewn, but that only added to their character. The stone sculptures were finely detailed and smooth. She could tell the wooden and stone sculptures were made by different artists, not just because of the materials, but also because they clearly had a different touch. There were multiple sculptures on display by the two artists. The pieces were affordable and made by unknown artists. Given the price of the sculptures and the time it likely took to make them, the artists were probably only barely making enough to live.

Okay, I choose you!

"Can I please buy these?"

She bought three wooden sculptures and four stone sculptures, which was the entire stock from each artist. The owner was quite surprised, but he seemed delighted about the sales. Not because he made money, but because two artists he's been rooting for were appreciated.

The sculptures were a little too heavy for Mitsuha to carry all at once, so she requested delivery. She could've jumped them but she'd have to carry them to a secluded spot first, and she would definitely draw a lot of attention to herself as she struggled to do so.

Sweet! That completes today's mission!

Mitsuha would be calling herself a sculptor while reselling the works of other artists, but it was kind of her only choice. If she called herself an art dealer, she'd have to explain where she got each item from and how much she paid for them. She wouldn't be able to say that she imported them from abroad. Claiming she bought them in Japan could get her into tax trouble. That left her with no choice but to claim that the business owner and sculptor Mitsuha Yamano was the maker of her merchandise.

That's why I'm selling the sculptures under the name Colette's Sculptures instead of my real name. I never explicitly said I made them!

One of the benefits of selling art was that Mitsuha could charge whatever she wanted for each item without complaint. Then again, she's the one buying them, so she's not exactly stealing any credit from the artists. The plan was to obtain a second citizenship in another country. Once she bought the art pieces for high prices as a foreigner, she would resell each one for a reasonable price with the real creator's name displayed. The artists deserved that small courtesy.

The resale price would be significantly cheaper than the prices at Colette's Sculptures, of course. That price tag wouldn't come close to what she originally paid for considering the exchange rate, but the artists would surely rather have their items sold for cheap—or market value price on Earth, rather—than stored away forever.

Once the sculptures were delivered to Mitsuha's General Store, she jumped them right to Japan. She snapped pictures of them with her digital camera and finished preparing her website.

The following day—for the first time in ages—Mitsuha went out to promote her store. She made her rounds to greet her neighbors and the orphanage to let them know she was back from her long trip. The shop was barely open an hour before she had to brave a hectic raid from all the women who had run out of shampoo and body wash. Shortly after the rush calmed down, a man walked in.

"Excuse me," he asked, "is this Viscountess Mitsuha von Yamano's mansion?"

Bffrt! Y-Yeah, that's my name and this is definitely my capital residence, but nobody's ever called me that or my house a mansion. I suppose he didn't want to call it my "house," and if he's here as a visitor to the viscountess rather than a customer to the store, I guess he had to call it that.

He doesn't look like a noble or a merchant at all. He was a tall, thin man who looked to be in his mid-twenties. *What business could he have with me as a viscountess rather than as the shop owner?*

"Thank you very much for buying my works," he said.

Oh, he's one of the sculptors! He went out of his way to thank the person who bought his art. He must've been so happy... But this can't be the first time he's ever sold something. Does he do this with everyone?

"There's no need to thank me. They're fine sculptures, and I was happy to purchase them, Mister, um…" Mitsuha trailed off.

"Ah, my name is Lortor."

Oh yeah, I remember that now. Each work in the art shop had been labeled with the artist's name to help them get recognized and gain repeat customers, but Mitsuha had forgotten it.

They talked for a little while about nothing in particular. Lortor seemed oddly restless, eyeing Mitsuha's every reaction. He showed no signs of leaving even when they began to talk in circles. Just as she was starting to get fed up, the front door opened again.

"Is this Viscountess Yamano's mansion?" A timid-looking woman stepped into the store. Contrary to her words, she seemed to know who she was speaking to. She continued without waiting for an answer, "Thank you so much for buying my art! Would you consider supporting me as a patron?"

Huh? Oh yeah, I suppose a lot of artists in this industry rely on patrons. It makes sense that they'd pounce at a once-in-a-lifetime opportunity to gain a noble as a patron after I'd just bought their works.

"Hey, I got here first! Wait your turn!" Lortor snapped.

"You can't tell me what to do! My livelihood depends on this!"

"Oh, screw off! I'm in the same boat!"

Oh brother. They've started fighting…

"Easy… Easy there…" Mitsuha appeased.

The two froze in place, realizing what they'd just done. Starting a shouting match in front of their potential patron was hardly any way for an artist to behave. Projecting an air of elegance in front of their benefactors was one of the jobs an artist had. Revealing the ugly reality of being a struggling artist would ruin the image. They understood that well, which was why they froze.

"…Haha, that was a joke! Moving on. Let's not ignore Viscountess Yamano." Lortor said to his rival.

"Y-Y-Yes, just messing around as usual, but that's enough of that…"

Man, these two have no shame…

"…So once again, I would love to have your patronage."

"As would I…"

They've decided to team up… Well, whatever. Doesn't matter to me.

The two artists were apparently acquaintances and rivals, which made sense given they sold their art in the same shop. Neither one could support themselves as full-time sculptors, and they struggled financially as they worked day jobs to stay afloat. They both dreamed of finding a patron and gaining prestige as an artist. It was a constant grind.

That was until one day, the owner of the art shop brought some news to them.

"A young noble girl bought all of your works. She must've really liked them. It was the Lightning Archpriestess, believe it or not."

"Holy crap, she's really famous! Nothing would get me greater publicity than working as the Archpriestess's personal sculptor!"

The two artists rushed right to their buyer's capital residence after hearing the news. Lortor had planned to open with a chat and naturally bring up the idea of Mitsuha supporting him. He took too long to do so, however, and was upstaged when his rival barged in and threw the question at her point blank. This sent Lortor into a frenzy, fearing that he was going to lose his patron. They were both usually gentle-mannered people. Allegedly.

Well, I suppose even the most good-natured person can lose it when their livelihood is at stake. Maybe even Gandhi would come charging red-eyed if he was in their situation.

Hmm. Becoming their patron would mean supporting them finan-

cially. That'd be difficult to stop once you start. If I were to suddenly pull my support after they become full-time artists, their lives would fall apart. Also, if I become their patron, no one else will support them out of fear of meddling with "my artists."

I don't like their art that much. I only thought their sculptures looked like the works of new artists with potential. They're hardly masterpieces. I have to be honest here…

"…Sorry. I can't support you," Mitsuha confessed.

"HUUUH?!" The artists were dumbstruck.

I really am sorry.

"P-Please reconsider!" Lortor panicked.

"You can support me just a little! I would love to have you as a patron, Archpriestess!" bargained the woman whose name was Tiras.

They initially addressed Mitsuha as a potential noble patron, but it was clear what they were really after: the name value of the Lightning Archpriestess. Even a small amount of support from Mitsuha would enable them to call her a patron, which would change the way everyone saw them. There was a chance other nobles and entrepreneurs would approach them as a gateway to the famed viscountess.

That's an all-win for them. There's just one problem—I really hate that kind of thing.

"No. If I support you, you'll be inundated with people trying to use you to get to me. You'll do well financially, but would you really be happy if your art sells not because of your own ability, but because of my name? I know your lives are hard right now, but will you be able to stomach that as artists?"

Lortor and Tiras fell silent. Their expressions were dark.

Ah, I feel kinda bad about the way I worded that. Hmm… How about this?

"Um, I actually have an unrelated request for you two…"

"Huh?" they both uttered. It was probably odd to have their customer ask something of them right after refusing to provide patronage. The word *request* suggested she wasn't ordering art, either.

"Honestly, I want to sell your sculptures that I bought in my home country. I don't want anyone in my country to know I'm involved, so I'm going to sell them to art dealers without displaying your names or mentioning this country. The art dealers will credit you as the artist when they resell your works. Do I have your permission to sell them that way?"

I'm not passing off their art as someone else's work, and they will be credited in the end. Hopefully they're okay with that...

"I don't mind at all! That sounds wonderful!"

"I-I'm fine with that too!"

Ah, just as I hoped. I'm going to regularly sell their art in another country. This is no different from a foreign art broker offering to regularly purchase the works of a new and nameless Japanese painter. Nobody would turn down such an offer.

All right, that's settled!

"Oh, keep in mind that having your works sold in my country won't spread your name here at all. You'll never gain fame if I'm your only customer," Mitsuha warned.

They both grimaced.

This might raise their spirits!

"Of course, I don't mind you telling people that Viscountess Yamano buys your art. That's nothing but the truth."

Lortor's and Tiras's faces lit up. Even if Mitsuha wasn't a patron, just having her as a customer could serve as very effective advertising.

Mitsuha wasn't originally planning to ask for the artists' approval before selling their works. No art dealer would ever seek out the artist's permission for every single piece of art that passed through their business. But if these two were happy to give their consent, that can only be a good thing.

Finally, my money exchange system is in place! All I have to do now is open a small art shop in one of the countries where I'll have citizenship.

Mitsuha had no desire to peddle to art dealers, so she was going to open a small art shop of her own that doubled as a café. The art would be sold at prices close to what she acquired them for. She would use the café to finance the shop's maintenance costs. Losing a little bit of money wasn't going to be a problem. Given her status as an honorary citizen, she wouldn't have to pay taxes even if she did make money. Small countries were nice and accommodating like that.

Of course, she had no intention of running the shop herself. She was going to leave it all up to a hired manager.

It would be nice to set up art around the café seating. Oh, I could call it a gallery café, and decorate it with all kinds of art instead of just sculptures! I can see myself now, sitting in the corner and pretending to be a regular customer as I sip my tea and admire the art... Yup, this is going to be good!

In the event of an emergency, leaving Japan and moving there would be an option. I could get rid of the money-bleeding art gallery, convert that space into ordinary seating, and make a living running a normal café. Not all of my hideouts need to be secret bases located far from human civilization. I can set up normal places to live too.

I'm getting excited!

The two young sculptors left Mitsuha's General Store. They didn't achieve their ultimate goal of patronage, but the store owner seemed like she'd buy more after having just purchased all of their pieces. They would be able to tell people that the Archpriestess was their frequent buyer, and that their work was well-received in her home country. A killer sales pitch. This filled them with hope for the future, something they couldn't have imagined just a day earlier when they lived paycheck to paycheck.

There were plenty of people who escaped poverty after grinding for years, believing in their talent, until luck finally came to them. But there were hundreds—no, thousands—more people who never got that chance and were crushed by the weight of their circumstances.

The two sculptors stopped a few steps outside of Viscountess Yamano's residence and shared a firm handshake. They were both beaming.

Chapter 40: Side Story
If Pearls are a Weapon, Iris Will Rule the World

"Oh no…"

Count Bozes, who was staying in his capital residence for ballroom season, grimaced and paused from his paperwork when he spotted a letter.

"Don't tell me…"

It was a party invitation from Marquis Tinoberque's wife. It was addressed to Count and Countess Bozes. That was fine on its own; they received such invitations all the time.

The problem was that Iris and Marchioness Tinoberque got along like cats and dogs.

Count Bozes's relationship with both Marquis and Marchioness Tinoberque was just fine. The same could be said for Marquis Tinoberque and the Bozes couple. They were actually quite friendly, and the two men had a lot in common as lords of their respective houses, and as nobles belonging to the same faction.

However, Countess Bozes and Marchioness Tinoberque… This was a different story. A very different story.

Perhaps it started when they were classmates at the same all-girls' school for nobles in the capital. Or maybe it was when Count Bozes proposed to Iris right before Marchioness Tinoberque's eyes—this was before she met the marquis.

Marriages among nobles were normally arranged between families regardless of how the wedded pair felt about it. It was very rare for a noble to propose directly to another. The youngest child of a low-ranking noble may get away with making such advances, but certainly not the heir to a count's family. Count Bozes's proposal naturally caused a big commotion, and many young ladies of the nobility were jealous of Iris.

The all-girls' school Iris went to was technically a school, but it was really just an institution where nobles' daughters were temporarily sent to get acquainted with people other than their family and servants. Their actual education and noble training were carried out by vassals, servants, and private tutors at home. It was really nothing more than a place to socialize.

Having said that, it was also a terrifying place where the girls got a direct sense for the factions and power dynamics in noble society. And whatever happened in the girls' school stayed in the girls' school. No woman who went there ever spoke of it to a man.

It seemed pretty different from the boys' school Count Bozes attended, where the students trained at the sword, had dumb fun, and made lifelong friends and connections. Count Bozes had asked his wife about the girls' school many times, but she never told him anything.

Anyway, Marchioness Tinoberque and Iris couldn't have gotten along worse. If they both attended a debutante ball or birthday party of a mutual acquaintance's child, or any important party, they simply ignored each other and got through the evening without incident. They at least had that amount of self-control.

But anytime they met at a party where they didn't have to be considerate of other families or children, drama was in tow. And to Count Bozes's chagrin, the Tinoberques were hosting a party for the marchioness's birthday. She'd be on her own turf, free from the concern of ruining another family's party. There was no way she was going to hold back. Iris sure wouldn't either.

Count Bozes grew stressed as the image of a dragon fighting a manticore against a backdrop of flames formed in his mind.

"Of course I'm going."

"Wha..."

Maybe she'll turn down the invitation. I hope she turns down the invitation. Actually, she'll probably turn down the invitation, Count Bozes had been praying, but he was dejected by Iris's response.

"I won't have Marchioness Tinoberque thinking I ran from a fight on a disadvantageous field."

"A fight, you say..." Count Bozes muttered as all hope of preventing an incident wilted within him. *Iris is as Iris does.*

She continued, "All you have to do on a disadvantageous battlefield is prepare a weapon to turn the situation in your favor."

"A weapon?"

Count Bozes had no idea what his wife meant. But from her malicious grin, he knew full well she was up to no good...

Noble parties weren't like Japanese parties, which began with a formal toast only after everyone arrived. Instead, guests flowed in steadily over time and formed into groups that chatted amongst themselves, and after a while of mingling, the host would welcome everyone. This system made sense in a society where people traveled by horse-drawn carriage, which made it difficult to arrive on schedule.

Arriving exactly on time was considered rude, even. The common etiquette was that a guest should arrive a little late. And here at the Tinoberques' party, it was about time for all the guests to have arrived.

"Greetings, everyone! Welcome to my birthday party!" Marchioness Tinoberque announced after being escorted to the stage by her husband. Count Bozes looked at Iris, expecting to see a loathsome expression as she gazed at the star of the party, but instead, she looked strangely at ease. This only made him more anxious.

Iris looked beautiful in her simple low-cut dress and flowy shawl. Her appearance hardly changed from when he first met her. As Count Bozes marveled at his wife, Marchioness Tinoberque finished her speech and walked directly toward them.

Here we go... There's nothing I can do, he thought, resigning himself to the inevitable. Marquis Tinoberque followed behind his wife, looking just as perturbed as the count.

"Oh my. You came to celebrate my birthday, Countess Bozes? I'm flattered." They never used each other's first names, despite being former classmates.

"Why, of course. When I heard you were turning another year older, I just knew I had to be here to witness it. Ohohoho!"

A vein twitched in Marchioness Tinoberque's temple.

"Oh, how kind of you! Ohohoho!"

"Ohohohohoho!" the two women laughed together.

The guests around them all fell silent, looking supremely uncomfortable.

As Count Bozes stared at the interaction with the gaze of a dead fish, he thought with great sincerity: *I want to go home...*

"Oh, I must show you the birthday present my husband gave me," Marchioness Tinoberque said. She removed her shawl—which she wore the same way Iris was wearing hers—to reveal her neckline.

"Wow!" the guests all gasped in unison.

It was a pendant with a brilliant red gem. The gem's color, size, and total lack of impurities would've made it fit for a queen. Marchioness Tinoberque lifted the gem so everyone would be able to see it and held it right before Iris's eyes, not even trying to be casual about it. She beamed triumphantly.

Marchioness Tinoberque had never once mentioned the difference in rank between their husbands during her fights with Iris. Those ranks belonged to their husbands and had nothing to do with their own merits. This, however, was fair game. The gem was hers to wear, and it was proof that she had the charm to inspire her husband to give her such gifts. It was proof of her own finesse.

But Marchioness Tinoberque's expression quickly clouded with a sense of doubt. She had expected to revel in Iris's frustration, but the woman remained calm. She even smiled slightly.

Iris had known this was coming. It was for this moment that she'd given her young maids allowances along with an order to "become friends with the Tinoberque family's maids and report back the gossip." She even offered to reimburse the maids for all the money they spent carrying out their mission, separate from their allowances. The maids jumped at the chance to go to candy stores and cosmetic shops for free.

They aligned their breaks with those of the Tinoberque servants, casually approached them, and used their funds to buy them sweets. They bonded rather quickly. The Tinoberque servants spilled the tea: their master's wife was ecstatic after convincing her husband to buy her an incredible gem despite his consternation over the hefty price tag.

Iris used this information to plan a counterattack.

"Oh, how nice. My husband gave me a gift as well. It wasn't even my birthday…" Iris removed her shawl to unveil an accessory of her own.

Silence. The room felt fearsomely quiet. What she wore around her neck shouldn't exist. It looked like something a goddess should wear. No, that wasn't quite right—it was something *only* a goddess should wear. It was a miraculous necklace made with almost perfectly spherical pearls of exquisite size and color.

Victory! Iris thought. The corners of her lips curled upward as she observed the astonishment on Marchioness Tinoberque's face.

"Wh-Wh-What is that…" the woman choked.

"Oh, it's just a pearl necklace. My husband doesn't even wait for special occasions to give me such gifts."

The marchioness was speechless, and the other ladies at the party took the opportunity to barrage Iris with questions.

"Wh-Where did your husband buy that?!"

Iris answered, "He said someone gave it to him as repayment for a favor. He's always so kind."

"Wh-Who was it?! Tell me their name!"

"He only gave us an alias. We don't know his real name."

"Excuse me, Count Bozes. Would you be willing to introduce me to the gentleman who gave you that necklace?"

"How much did you pay for it?"

Meanwhile, Count Bozes was being hounded by the counts, marquises, and dukes. They knew what their wives would demand of them as soon as they got home, and wanted to get as much information as they could.

The value of the necklace was obvious. But if Count Bozes was able to obtain one, they thought there was a chance, no matter how small, that it was within their reach too. The necklace was so luxurious it shouldn't exist. But here existed one, right before their eyes. It was natural to assume there could be more.

Those with the rank of viscount or lower couldn't bring themselves to join in on the probing. They knew a necklace like that was out of their reach, no matter how much their wives pestered them for it. They wanted to at least hear how much Count Bozes paid for it, though, so they could convince their wives to give up hope.

But Count Bozes couldn't tell them the truth. After all, he only paid for it by purchasing a building for Mitsuha in the capital, funding its remodeling, and giving her a little cash for the road before she left his county. He received a national-treasure tier pearl necklace for next to nothing.

He knew what people would say about the Bozes family if he shared that story.

"They're wicked people who deceived and stole the family heirloom of a foreign girl."

"The Bozeses are a shame to Zegleus."

"Those fiends disgust me."

There was nothing Count Bozes could say that would convince them that he truly didn't deceive her. He wouldn't have believed himself if he were in their shoes and may have even accused the man in his position as a con.

The Bozeses actually intended to return the necklace when Mitsuha repaid the loan. Either that or give it back to her when she got married, calling it a wedding gift. The count hoped she would marry into his family, but even if she chose someone else, he intended to give the necklace to her all the same.

But he couldn't say a word of that now. Instead, he told the story that he and Iris had prepared for such an occasion. They cleared the story with Mitsuha too.

The story went as follows:

One day, seven men reached the shores of Bozes County in a small boat. They said their ship was wrecked at sea, and evacuated onto the small boat.

One of the men was luxuriously dressed and behaved like a lord. The other six men seemed to be his guards. Count Bozes invited the men to his mansion and offered them his hospitality. A few days later when they decided on their departure, the count gave them supplies and sufficient travel expenses for a long journey to cross the land. The lord bestowed him the pearl necklace as a token of his appreciation.

The lord was probably a man of noble birth from a distant country. He couldn't stand departing without rewarding Count Bozes for his generous hospitality, and the necklace was all he had to give. His attendants tried fervently to stop him from giving up the necklace, and Count Bozes firmly refused it, but the lord just smiled casually, forced it into his hands, and left.

That was the story. They couldn't possibly claim that he bought the necklace at its proper value. That would lead people to wonder where he got the money. It was worth more than a national treasure, and while Count Bozes was an influential noble for his position, he was still a count from a rural region. This necklace wasn't something he could buy on a whim.

Not even tax evasion, a hidden fortune, or embezzlement of his county's budget would explain how he was able to afford such a priceless item. That left finding a gold mine in his county, smuggling, a backdoor deal with another nation... He couldn't even imagine what terrible things others would suspect him of. He had no choice but to claim that he happened to obtain the necklace for close to no cost.

Count Bozes was a shrewd lord and noble, but his reputation for being hopelessly kind in his personal life lent his story credibility. Nobody doubted his claim. But their desire to know the identity of the travelers across the sea and their jealousy towards Count Bozes's good fortune only made them lose their composure even more.

The noble ladies all crowded around Iris to admire the "Goddess's necklace," as they began to call it. Their husbands surrounded Count Bozes to debate the identity of the mysterious men, the origins of the necklace, and whether it was the only one of its kind. Everyone was having a grand time.

…Everyone except Marchioness Tinoberque—who was left all alone, and her birthday totally forgotten.

It's been seven days since the Tinoberques' party. Iris was still in a great mood after the savage blow she delivered to her rival. Count Bozes approached her with a tense expression.

"…His Majesty the King invited us to a dinner party tomorrow."

"Huh?"

Her reaction was understandable. Official meetings with the king could come at short notice, but invitations for parties or banquets were usually delivered at least a month in advance. This allowed guests to prioritize the event and avoid making other plans. It also gave noble ladies enough time to buy new clothing and accessories, diet, and tend to their skin.

This time, the king's invitation to Count Bozes was verbal, not by a formal letter. With only a day's notice.

That was absolutely, positively unthinkable.

"…How many people will be at the banquet?" Iris asked.

There was no way the king could hold a normal banquet on such short notice. Iris figured it was likely to be a small-scale affair with a limited number of attendees. It was a massive honor for the lord of a rural territory to be invited to such an event.

"Just us two."

"What?"

"You and I are the only people invited. It will be a simple, informal dinner party instead of a banquet. His Majesty has commanded that you wear the pearl necklace."

"HUUUUH?!" It was a rare moment where Iris lost her composure.

"Th-Thank you very much for the invitation, Your Majesty," Iris greeted.

"No need to thank me!" the king laughed. "This is not a formal dinner. Except for the waiters, we'll be all alone. Be at ease."

Iris was born into a noble family. She had quite a presence at the girls' school, and she had met the king before. But greeting the king with a stock phrase as one attendee of many at a large party was much different than sitting down to an exclusive dinner. She could hardly be expected to keep her cool.

The woman sitting next to the king exhibited none of his courtliness. It was the queen, and her piercing gaze was fixed on Iris's neck.

I knew it... Iris and Count Bozes both thought. They figured the necklace would be the reason for the invitation, given the king's instruction for Iris to wear it.

The queen popped the question just as they started eating. She couldn't wait any longer.

"Um, where did you get that necklace...?"

It was likely that the queen had already heard the story of how

Count Bozes obtained the necklace when she first learned of its existence. But she probably thought he made the story up to hide what really happened. But the Bozeses repeated the same tale they told at the party.

"Do you truly have no clues that could point to their identity?" the queen asked.

"That is right. They thanked me many times, but never told me anything about themselves."

"I see…"

The queen looked disheartened, but she wasn't going to give up that easily. There was a high chance it was the only necklace of its kind, anyway. It was unbelievable enough that even one existed.

"Th-Then, could I—"

"Hmm, I suppose obtaining another of the same necklace would be impossible." The interruption came from the king. "It may have been a gift from the Goddess to reward you, Bozes, for your kindness toward those strangers."

Not even the queen could force someone to talk who didn't want to, and it would be quite problematic if she went so far as to demand the Bozeses give her the necklace. Count Bozes received the necklace as payment for his kindness, and by now it was well known that he had given it to his wife. If the queen were to be seen wearing it, it would seem like the king and queen summoned a noble and forced him to give up a priceless jewel that he received as a sign of thanks and gifted to his wife. The royal family's authority would plummet.

Even if the Bozeses refused to give it up, just the fact that the queen demanded it at a private dinner would be lethal. Any time the king or queen were to do something that seemed to belittle the Bozeses, the other nobles would think they were harassing them as punishment for not handing over the necklace.

Damn it! The king was just realizing how majorly he messed up. The Bozeses' new treasure, touted as the Goddess's necklace, was dominating conversation in high society. He invited Count Bozes and his wife to a private dinner because the queen begged him for the chance to see it.

If the king and queen attended the birthday party of a marquis's wife, there would be no end to the other parties they'd have to attend. The oldest son's birthday party, the second oldest son's birthday party, and the parties of other marquis's families... They'd have to juggle multiple parties a day.

The king explained this to the queen who wanted to attend birthday parties, and turned down all the invitations. As a result, she ended up missing out on the biggest topic of conversation among the nobility: the Goddess's necklace. The king relented to his wife's tearful woe and invited the Bozeses to dinner. He didn't even consider the potential consequences of that action.

The king stole a look at Count Bozes to see the man smiling widely.

"Your Majesty, I'm thinking of asking for your support at the meeting in three days regarding the development of the northern border region. I would appreciate it if you could arrange that for me..."

Countess Bozes was also smiling widely.

I've been had! the king seethed.

Count Bozes had a reputation for being hopelessly kind in his personal life, but as an influential noble and lord of the northern border region, he was quite the strategist. His wife, Iris, had quite the wile as well...

Chapter 41:
Monster Hunting

"Would you be willin' to take on a monster extermination job for me? I really need this!"

"Huh?"

This was not the front desk of an adventurers' guild in a world of swords and magic. Neither was the person begging a guild master.

"Where's this coming from, Captain?" Mitsuha asked.

This was a mercenary base on Earth in the 21st century. Not the typical place one would expect to land a monster hunting gig.

"You know how we offed those two dragons?" started the captain. "Two of my men were on vacation at the time and missed it, and the poor guys've been depressed ever since. I'm worried I'm gonna lose 'em if I can't find some way to cheer 'em up."

"Why is that my problem?!"

After her two-and-a-half-month campaign trip, Mitsuha returned Colette to her home for a break and set about taking care of some personal matters. The Wolf Fang mercenary base was her last stop.

I popped over here a few times during the trip, though, so it hasn't been six weeks since I've seen these guys. It's only been a few days.

The captain brought up the odd request shortly after she showed up.

"I'm beggin' you! You gotta know how they feel, right? Put yourself in their shoes. It'd be goddamn miserable!"

Urk! Yeah, if all my classmates teleported to another world and had a grand adventure they'd remember forever, and I missed it because I overslept... And I had to hear them talk about all the fun they had over and over again... Would I be able to enjoy my school life?

No way! It'd be absolutely impossible!

"Fine, I'll do it..."

Like I have any choice!

"How was your break? Did you have fun?" Mitsuha asked Colette after jumping to her village. The girl seemed hesitant.

Huh? Not quite the reaction I expected...

"The toilets here... And the bath... My *bed*... And the food! —Mrfm!"

Mitsuha scrambled to cover Colette's mouth but she was too late. Colette's parents were looking their way worriedly.

Sorry, guys. Colette might not be cut out for village life anymore...

Mitsuha gave Colette's parents ham, smoked cheese, and metal farming tools as gifts, which made them happy enough to seemingly forget about what Colette just said. *Thank goodness. They really are a simple-mind—ahem, I mean, easygoing folk.*

Colette gave them some of the wages she'd been saving up, which also made them very happy. This village barely had any cash income.

...I'm worried a bunch of other girls from this village are gonna ask me to hire them too. I can't bring them to my county without permission from their local lord, though. That would be unlawful pilfering of

citizens.

Mitsuha jumped back to her general store in the capital with Colette and unlocked the shop from the inside. While they waited for customers to arrive, she decided to do a little probing.

"Hey, are there a lot of monsters in our county? And do you know any places where we need to thin out some orcs or ogres?"

What sword do you use to cull monsters?

...Ex-cull-ibur!

Sorry, that was really bad...

Anyway, I need to know if there's a good hunting ground in my county.

"Nope," Colette said.

Oh, we don't have monsters... Wait, what?!

"Yamano County is a super small county between the mountains and the coast. Even the trails and forests are safe enough for children to explore. The hunters mainly hunt horned rabbits, foxes, bears, and boars. There *might* be a few goblins, kobolds, and orcs deep in the woods. But if some outlanders killed them for fun, they'd be stealing work from the hunters."

"Huh..."

Now that Mitsuha thought about it, she never received any reports of monster damage in her county. Come to think of it, monster-related concerns or safety measures never crossed her mind. Not having many monsters was a good thing, but it wasn't exactly what she wanted to hear right now.

"Hmm... What should I do, then..."

Seeing her friend in a pickle, Colette offered, "There are a whole bunch of monsters near my village. Goblins, orcs, ogres, boars, and even wolves!"

Wolves, huh... Oh no, my left arm is throbbing. The demon sealed within me is trying to break loose!

…Come on, Mitsuha! This isn't the time for cringey middle-school fantasies!

"Oh, that's good… Wait, no it's not! Is your village okay, Colette?!"

"If you get attacked by monsters, that just means you were unlucky or not careful enough."

"You're being way too casual about that!"

…But I guess that's how it is. They probably have to think that way. This place isn't safe like Japan; only the fittest survive in this world, and you never know when you could fall prey to something—or someone—stronger than you. People can be just as dangerous as monsters, if not more so.

"Well, let's go ask Count Bo—"

"I heard you're hunting monsters, Mitsuha!" A voice hollered out of nowhere.

"AAAH!" Mitsuha shrieked. *Where'd you come from, Sabine?!* "Don't get any ideas! I can't take a princess on a dangerous quest like this!"

"First things first. We'll have to form a party—"

"Are you listening to me?!"

With no sign of stopping—and her bodyguard standing behind her with a look of defeat—the princess barreled on. "Colette can fight up front as our warrior. I'll be the mage in the back…" Sabine glanced at Mitsuha. "You can be the gadabout, Mitsuha."

"Huh? Why?!"

I work harder than you and Colette combined! If anyone here should be a gadabout, it's you, Sabine!

Oh well, the king won't approve of this anyway. There's no way a lowly viscountess could get away with taking a princess to another county and allowing her to fight dangerous monsters without her father's permission. And getting his permission is not my job; it's Sabine's.

I know he has trouble saying no to her, but this crosses the line. I've got nothing to worry about here.

"Father, my last victory brought me to seventy-three points total. I wish to spend ten of those points to join a monster-hunting mission in Bozes County!"

"WHAAAAAAT?!" the king and Mitsuha screeched in unison.

What the hell, Sabine?!

The king nodded with tears in his eyes.

What the hell, Your Majesty?!

"...So yeah, anyway, could you give me permission to go hunt some monsters in Bozes County?"

"Don't 'yeah, anyway' me..." Count Bozes huffed, baffled by Mitsuha's request. "Do you understand what my entire family's fate would be if anything were to happen to Princess Sabine... If she received so much as one scratch?"

His face was deadly serious.

Oh yeah, it's not just my life that might be on the line if this goes badly... But it's all good. I've got it covered!

"Don't worry! I have a letter from His Majesty!"

"What..."

It was a handwritten letter from the king declaring that the princess was participating in the hunt by her own insistence, and no one with her would be held responsible for any accidents unless ill intent is suspected. Sabine spent two points to get her father to write it.

I'm gonna need to ask her exactly how that point system works.

Wait, no! Bad idea! What if she demands a point system from me too?! And then racks up a ton of points... That would be AWFUL!

Yeah, I'm better off forgetting about this...

"So, if it's no inconvenience to you, could you please grant Princess Sabine's request?"

Count Bozes couldn't refuse after the king wrote him such a self-effacing letter. His expression grew more and more unpleasant as he read it.

"...Fine. I'll allow it. But I insist on assigning you guides and guards from my county!"

"Huh? Guards for a group of monster hunters? That's like assigning guards to protect soldiers..."

"I insist!"

"Yes sir..."

And so, our monster-hunting party was dispatched to Colette Village in Bozes County.

"That's not the name of the village, Mitsuha..."

Fine...

And here we are in Colette Village.

"Again, that's not the name of the village! Get it right, Mitsuha!" The complaint was from Colette.

Hmm, I guess I'd be embarrassed if someone called the town where I live "Mitsuha Town." All right, I'll make a mental note to pull some strings with the count and make him rename it to Colette Village.

Mitsuha wasn't acting as the lord of Yamano County on this hunt, so Colette was in friend mode. That's why she was calling her "Mitsuha" instead of "Viscountess Yamano." Sabine called her "Mitsuha" regardless of whether she was in princess or friend mode, despite the girl's initial desire to call her "Mistress Mitsuha" out of respect. Mitsuha didn't want people to think she was forcing a princess to humble herself around her.

The hunting party consisted of Mitsuha, Colette, Sabine, the Wolf Fang captain and two of his men, plus…

"Count Bozes, Lady Iris, Alexis, and Theodore? What are you doing here?"

I don't know if I should be glad that Beatrice isn't here, or scared for later…

"I told you I was going to assign guides and guards," Count Bozes said matter-of-factly. Trailing behind him was a hunter whom Mitsuha knew from the village…along with thirty soldiers.

"This is overkill! You even gave the guards four additional people to protect!" protested Mitsuha.

Hey, I'll yell at a count if he deserves it. I don't care.

"I told you I'm doing this because some divine soldiers from my home country wanted to experience hunting monsters! If all of us herd into the forest, the monsters will flee!" She was livid.

Mitsuha had explained to the count that the king of her home country sent these three soldiers because he wanted them to test the effectiveness of divine weapons against monsters at close range. During the last battle at the capital, the soldiers only mowed down monsters from a distance. *By the way, I said that monsters were wiped out in my part of the land a long time ago.*

Mitsuha also told the count that the soldiers traveled here on a small high-speed boat. The three Wolf Fang mercenaries already knew that she could transport much more at a time with her world-jumping ability than she told the national representatives of Earth.

I kinda told them myself, actually. I don't want them trying to prevent me from using my power if I ever need to get reinforcements or mass-transport weapons or supplies in an emergency. I might need to borrow a light armored vehicle at some point. Do I know how to drive one, you ask? Of course! As long as the seats are adjustable enough for me to reach the pedals…

A 5.56 mm caliber light machine gun won't have enough firepower, though. That would work against humans, but not against monsters. I'd rather have a reconnaissance combat vehicle with a 25 mm caliber autocannon and a 7.62 mm caliber light machine gun, or an armored combat vehicle with a 35 mm caliber autocannon… Wait, what kind of enemy is Yamano County gonna be fighting with these things?!

Anyway, Mitsuha had Count Bozes dismiss some of the guards. The three Wolf Fang mercenaries could protect the group on their own, and Mitsuha and the girls were armed with pistols. They didn't need guards. The Bozeses should have some security, but she could just jump them to safety in an emergency; having enough manpower to hold off a surprise attack for a few seconds was enough. They ended up taking four guards, one for each of the Bozeses, and the rest were back at the village on standby.

We don't see much around here, aside from some ogres, anyway. People would never choose to live anywhere near dangerous monsters like dragons or manticores. If anything like that was sighted, the village would either be deserted by now or it'd be bustling with the royal army's extermination branch or hunters hoping to make a kill and get rich.

Count Bozes was greatly opposed to reducing the number of guards, but he finally relented when Mitsuha asked if he wanted to make the soldiers who came all this way have to report to their king that the mission failed because they had too many guards and scared the monsters away. He had no argument when he pictured himself in their shoes.

None of the Bozeses had seen the gunfire during the battle to defend the capital. Count Bozes was still heading to the capital with his county army, Alexis was in a hospital on Earth, and Iris and Theodore were back home. Alexis didn't even see Mitsuha fire her gun when she killed the assassin during the military council; he'd collapsed after jumping in front of her and taking those arrows. He heard the gunshots, though. Considering that, the Bozeses probably tagged along because they wanted to see the might of the divine weapons. They were testing the guns on the invasive ships from the kingdom of Vanel, but surely they've heard that the divine weapons were much more powerful.

Oh, what about the M1 Garland, you ask? I didn't give a demonstration in this kingdom. There's no need to flaunt the power of guns to the people here. I have their trust already. So yeah, the Bozeses probably forced their way into this hunt just to watch the show—er, to "gather information." Well, it's not like I mind.

The hunt was on. The hunter from Colette Village (name pending) led the group, followed by the three Wolf Fang mercenaries, Mitsuha and the girls, the Bozeses, and finally, the four guards. There were fifteen people in total. *That's still way too many!*

We have three—Iris, Alexis, and Theodore—who aren't fit for combat. That's not ideal. The hunter should be able to fight, of course, and the girls and I have our Walthers.

The monsters are gonna falter when they see our Walthers… Hey, shut up! Can't a girl have some fun?!

"Don't insult me and Alexis like that! We're noble men! Of course we can fight!" Theodore grumped.

Wait. What?

"…Did I say that out loud?" Mitsuha gulped.

"You've been talking aloud this whole time!"

Oh crap…

"Iris is stronger than me, you know?" muttered Count Bozes. *Huh? Did I just hear him right?!*

A few hours passed as the group hiked along a mountain trail.

"We should find some monsters soon."

Mitsuha translated the hunter's warning to the Wolf Fang mercenaries. They couldn't understand what he was saying.

It seemed like the hunter had spent the trek so far avoiding areas where monsters were sighted, which made sense. Shooting loud guns near the village would've scared away the local hunters' usual game. Orcs and other monsters were important prey, so killing them all would've caused problems for the villagers. Now that they were a few hours into the forest, a fleeing monster would likely take cover near the village. The hunter was doing a good job of turning this chore to his advantage.

Those monsters aren't gonna attack the village though, right? I'm a little worried...

The two Wolf Fang subordinates chose 7.62 mm caliber assault rifles as their main weapon. It was more common nowadays to use 5.56 mm caliber rifles with high-velocity bullets, but they went with the old-fashioned 7.62 mm bullet rifles because they were going to be firing them in a forest with a lot of vegetation, and because orcs and ogres had much thicker flesh than humans.

On the other hand, the captain stuck with a 5.56 mm caliber rifle to see how it did against monsters compared to a 7.62 mm. He was planning on testing various bullets too—normal, armor-piercing ammunition, etc. Mitsuha figured he was conducting research in case she gave him another job in the future.

...He's not planning on seeking out opportunities to fight monsters even when I don't have a job for him, is he? Well, I guess I don't mind

mediating for him if there's a county that's suffering from a monster problem.

Wait, what happened to my "traversal saps my life force" claim?! Geez, I forgot all about that for a second. I gotta stop making decisions based on my sympathies...

"We've got monsters!" The hunter spotted something.

The three Wolf Fang members seemed to understand without any translation and readied their assault rifles. They waited until they laid eyes on the target. They weren't jumpy amateurs who would accidentally shoot one of their own because grass moved or because they sensed something nearby. These guys were pros.

Six monsters emerged from behind the trees.

"Targets sighted!" exclaimed Mitsuha. "Goblins! I give you permission to attack!"

I told the Wolf Fang guys not to shoot without my permission unless it was an emergency. I'd feel awful if they shot an elf or a dwarf. I don't know if those exist in this world or not, but still.

Bang! Bang! Bang!

The blasts of the semi-automatic rifles echoed in the forest.

"Looks like 5.56 mm bullets are enough to take on goblins. They're about the same as humans... Actually, they're smaller and frailer, and don't wear armor either." The captain wasn't fazed because he'd seen goblin, orc, and ogre corpses before. As for the other two...

"That was lame!"

"I wanna shoot something stronger! Are there any bigger monsters?!"

They were completely unsatisfied.

Hey, don't be so ungrateful! I'll make you hunt horned rabbits next!

After walking a little further, they encountered three orcs.

We did find some rabbits too—their horns remind me of a certain mobile suit—but the two Wolf Fang subordinates turned their noses up at them. What a shame. Those rabbits are tasty.

The mercenaries readied their guns and faced the orcs.

"Fire!" the captain commanded.

The three rifles let out loud, crisp bangs. They were in semi-automatic mode; fully automatic would've been overkill against three targets. There was no way a professional mercenary would miss from this distance with assault rifles, especially when aiming at enemies that couldn't shoot back.

However...

"Shit, the 5.56 mm bullets ain't working!" the captain cursed. His 5.56 mm bullets weren't measuring up compared to the full-sized 7.62 mm battle rifle bullets. You could compensate for reducing the ammo weight against human opponents by increasing the speed of the bullet or changing its shape or material, but it turned out they didn't muster enough power to harm monsters that were tougher.

"Crap, these aren't doin' much!" one of the men yelled.

Well shoot, the 7.62 mm bullets aren't quite strong enough either.

They weren't completely ineffective, of course, but while one or two 7.62 mm bullets was enough to incapacitate a human, it was going to take a lot more to disable a monster.

It didn't help that the mercenaries were using full metal jacket bullets made for military use; the bullets were sturdy and rarely broke upon impact. The gunshot wound wasn't very severe. Orcs also had significantly bulkier muscles than any human. Even with full-size rifle bullets, you were going to need more than one or two shots to pierce their thick hides and inflict a mortal wound.

During the battle to defend the capital, the mercenaries used both light and heavy machine guns. They didn't take the time to assess each shot's efficiency when they were firing full-auto mode. Now, however, they were going to have to hit a vital spot to take the orcs down.

"Aim for their heads!"

That was the right call; if they couldn't pierce the orcs' chests, they just had to aim for a spot without bulk. It was highly unlikely that assault rifle bullets wouldn't be able to pierce their skulls.

The captain probably wanted to hit other parts of the orcs' bodies for research, but that wouldn't have been the safest thing to do as the monsters were sprinting toward them. They needed to finish them off immediately.

The mercenaries each fired twice for a total of six gunshots before the orcs fell to the ground.

"I guess assault rifles ain't strong enough for orcs…"

"Havin' to aim for the head's too limiting in most situations…"

"They might work if we used special bullets, but those ain't cheap…"

"Hmm. So if the li'l lady's home is attacked by a horde o' monsters, assault rifles and SAWs won't cut it…" the captain mulled.

Oh, they're not just doing this for fun. They're also testing to see how best to protect my county in the future! Sorry guys, I underestimated you.

Modern squad automatic weapons typically used 5.56 mm bullets compatible with assault rifles, so even with their rapid rate of fire, they wouldn't do enough damage to take down an orc. You could easily take out one orc by barraging it, but that wouldn't be practical in an all-out battle.

The Bozeses and the guards stared in awe, but the "lightning wands" that killed the orcs so easily were definitely not invincible.

"All right, let's keep going," said Mitsuha.

The hunter gave a longing glance at the game they were leaving behind, but he knew they couldn't carry the orcs all the way back to the village. Making the rest of the group carry them wasn't an option. Count Bozes had hired him as the guide. Even thinking about his own gains or slowing down the operation by carrying it himself was out of the question. He had to give it up. *I'll pay him later to make up for it,* Mitsuha thought.

The party continued deeper into the forest. Suddenly, something jumped out of the trees right in front of them.

"Ogres! A whole pack of them!" The hunter panicked.

Ogres were the strongest monsters that inhabited the area. And out of nowhere, there was a horde practically right on top of them.

The Wolf Fang mercenaries didn't miss a beat to shoot at their heads, but the bullets barely had any effect. The monsters blocked the ammo with their thick arms. One of the subordinates tried to switch out his empty magazine, but an ogre swung at him and knocked him off his feet. The other subordinate decided he didn't have time to reload his magazine and instead drew a pistol and fired desperately. The rifle bullets had no effect; pistol bullets had no chance.

Just when one of the ogres was about to swing his arm at the fallen man, the captain shot the rest of his 5.56 mm bullets at its head, killing it. Not even an ogre could take that many assault rifle bullets to the face.

More ogres were charging close behind the first one. The subordinate who was swept off his feet was still alive, but he hadn't recovered enough to stand. The captain and the other subordinate scrambled to reload their magazines, but they weren't fast enough. They had no choice but to block the ogres' punches with their rifles.

We need to run! No, I need to get Sabine and Colette out of here! Our pistols aren't gonna do any good. What should I do—

Mitsuha's panic was interrupted by the sound of something slicing through the air. When she looked up, she saw that the Bozeses had leapt in front of the mercenaries and swung their swords down. Eight blades *whooshed, swished,* and *sliced* as they tore up the orcs. Blood spattered all around them.

Yep, eight blades. All four Bozeses and their guards are fending off the ogres.

Men in the nobility led armies on the battlefield. They were trained to fight from a young age and, naturally, were stronger than the average soldier. Even Theodore was holding his own. The guards were also doing their best to support Alexis, Theodore, and Iris so they didn't get hurt.

Count Bozes didn't even need the guards' support. He was unquestionably more skilled than all of the guards—who were handpicked out of a group of thirty elite fighters all capable enough to serve the count's family.

I'm not surprised the count, Alexis, and Theodore are all so skilled. That's expected of noble men… But Lady Iris, how are you so strong?

Wow, she just cut another ogre's throat…

The mercenaries finished reloading their magazines as the Bozeses kept the ogres at bay. The subordinate who'd been knocked off his feet had rejoined the fight; he wasn't injured too badly. The captain's assault rifle had been rendered unusable, so he held a pistol in his right hand and a knife in his left.

The 7.62 mm bullets were more than enough to kill an ogre as long as there was enough time and distance to aim for a weak spot. The mercenaries were at point-blank range, and the ogres were distracted by the swords in front of them. A clear headshot was a cinch. The great height of the ogres also removed the risk of accidentally shooting an ally.

The mercenaries fired their guns until all the ogres fell.

"I thought we were goners..." the captain shuddered. The subordinates nodded, pale-faced. "I underestimated 'em. Assault rifles are enough to kill ogres if you hit a vital point, but those bastards can survive six shots to the chest and keep chargin'. We'd be toast if they surprise us from close range or surround us... We got lucky back there..."

During the battle to defend the capital, the mercenaries were far away from the monsters and had nothing to obstruct them as they mowed down the charging army. Their heavy machine guns gave the monsters no chance of coming anywhere near them. If a horde of beasts had surprised them at close range in a forest, they probably would've died.

The guards and the Bozeses are much more prepared for that kind of situation.

Two of the guards were injured protecting everyone. Fortunately, the wounds weren't life-threatening. They looked like serious injuries to Mitsuha and the others, but the guards seemed to consider them nothing more than scratches. They laughed casually as their companions tied up their wounds.

The guards had been truly gallant as they calmly brandished their blades against the giant ogres, dodged their swinging arms, and inflicted slash after slash. Each one was a man among men, worthy of being called a soldier. *It just hits different watching a person fight with his own physical prowess and spirit, unlike people on modern Earth who rely on the strength of their weapons!*

Without these guards, we'd all be—hold on, why didn't I jump us all away?! How could I have been that out of it?! Some of us could've died. I can't afford to make mistakes like that!

I froze out of fear.

I got cocky with this whole mission. I felt invincible. But once those ogres showed up, I totally blanked…

The Bozeses probably never once thought that I would jump them away. I doubt the idea occurred to the Wolf Fang guys either in the heat of battle. It's not something they're used to relying on. And I was the one who naively decided to shrink the number of our guards. My mistake put everyone in danger and let two guards get injured. I'm so stupid…

The wounded men were in a great mood, excited by the honor of protecting not just the Bozeses, but also the Archpriestess—the savior of their kingdom—and her divine soldiers. They reveled in their ability to carry out the Goddess's will with their own blades, without a need for the divine lightning wands. The Wolf Fang mercenaries, who looked dejected over their failure, looked up at the guards as if staring at gods.

Yeah, the guards just made them look like total wimps… And they were even upstaged by two children and a noble lady. Their dignity as divine soldiers must be in shambles…

"We're going back with traversal," announced Mitsuha.

"Huh?" The Bozeses were wide-eyed. Their reaction was unsurprising given what Mitsuha had said about her life force.

"I put you all in danger with my naivety. It's my fault the guards were injured, and I can't let them walk for hours in that state. I'll take you all back to the Bozes estate with traversal and take the hunter to Colette Village after that."

"For the last time, that's not the name of the village…"

Mitsuha ignored Colette's comment. *I'm sure that name will stick if I say it enough times. Persistence pays off.*

Colette and Sabine stayed back during that fight. They were probably too scared to do anything…just like me. We didn't stand much chance of hurting the ogres, but we could've helped to hold them back by shooting them in the face with our pistols. An accurate shot from close range might've killed or at least blinded one.

...But I was useless. I couldn't move. Why, though? I had no problem shooting the ancient dragons...

Mitsuha had heard that ancient dragons were more intelligent than humans. That might've been why she was able to remain calm as she faced them; it didn't feel much different than facing a human. Even though they were massive creatures who thought of humans as insects and killed without hesitation.

By contrast, ogres were brutal, mindless beasts driven only by their greed. Never had death felt so close. Mitsuha had frozen with fear, and the same probably went for Sabine and Colette. She could shoot people from a distance just fine, but when faced with monsters at close range, she was overwhelmed.

I was naive. Just stupid. I was so flustered I even forgot about jumping, nearly killing Sabine, Colette, and the three Wolf Fang mercenaries.

Don't I care about the Bozeses, you ask? They would've been fine. I think they would've wiped out the ogres easily, even without our help.

Arrgghh, damn it! Damn it, damn it, damn it! I'm such an idiot! That's why I have to do this...

"I'm not changing my mind," Mitsuha said hollowly, forcing down her turbulent emotions. Count Bozes and Lady Iris looked back at her with the same solemn expression. She would've expected them to yell at her so much that veins bulged in their temples, but they stood in silence.

...They can probably tell how I feel.

Alexis and Theodore looked at her with pity in their eyes. *I didn't think I was showing any emotion, but my frustration must still be really apparent... Whatever.*

"Gather around me." Everyone did as she asked without objection. "Jump!"

I guess I should've yelled "Traversal!" but that hardly matters...

Mitsuha jumped everyone to the Bozes estate. They didn't notice they were on Earth for a split-second in between. She left the Bozeses and the guards saying she would come back to apologize another day, then took everyone else to the Wolf Fang base on Earth. She left the mercenaries there, then went to Colette Village with the hunter, Colette, and Sabine. Finally, she jumped alone to retrieve the dead orcs and ogres.

"I'm giving you these in exchange for your word that you won't tell anyone what you saw today. If you do tell anyone..." Mitsuha paused suggestively. The hunter went pale under the weight of her blank stare and nodded fervently. It was evident that he wouldn't dare disclose the divine soldiers' failure or her ability to a soul.

I feel bad about threatening the hunter, but he saw too much. Well, these orcs and ogres combined with the reward he'll receive from the count will make for a sufficient reward/hush money.

Mitsuha dropped by Colette's house to greet her parents, then jumped to her home in Japan with the girls. They washed off their sweat and grime and went to bed in each other's arms.

It was the shortest bath they'd taken, and all three were silent the entire time. Mitsuha thought she could feel Sabine and Colette shivering in her arms. They couldn't be cold after taking a warm bath. *It's probably just my imagination.*

"Rise and shine!"

"Shut up, Mitsuha!"

"Yes, Mitsuha. Why are you yelling?!"

Yikes, that didn't go over well! I guess having someone shout in your ear isn't the most pleasant way to wake up.

"Where'd all this energy come from?" grumbled Sabine. "You were so depressed yesterday!"

I'm known for my ability to bounce back in a snap!

"Mwahaha, I'll reflect on my actions, but I won't dwell on them!"

"You can't be serious!"

Everyone makes mistakes in life! No point in letting it get me down!

Once everyone got out of bed, Mitsuha made a simple breakfast with leftovers in the fridge. She then jumped Sabine to the royal palace, Colette to her home in Yamano County, and lastly, herself to the Wolf Fang base. She didn't appear inside with no warning, of course; she appeared outside, out of view, and walked into the building where the captain's office was.

"Is Captain here?" Mitsuha asked one of the mercenaries who was hanging out.

"Yeah, he's doin' some kinda training outside."

That's unusual. The mercenaries never skimp on their training, but the captain always does his physical training in the afternoon. He doesn't like working out in the morning because of the temperature, muscle stiffness, and how he has to take a shower after he sweats, Mitsuha thought as she headed to where she was instructed.

She found the captain waving around what looked like a practice sword. He was joined by the two subordinates from yesterday along with some other men.

"...What are you doing?"

"Oh, it's the li'l lady! We're trainin' with the sword to prepare for next time. A real man wields a sword. Ain't that right, guys?" The two subordinates from yesterday nodded. "I got these practice swords right after we got back yesterday. We'll never get caught with our pants down like that again. You can count on us!"

Count Bozes, Lady Iris, Alexis, Theodore, and the four guards were undeniably epic yesterday. Using nothing but their skill and speed to fight off and overpower ogres with muscles so thick they could repel assault rifle bullets—they were practically heroes. What they did shouldn't have been humanly possible. They were soldiers worthy of their position as the protectors of the border territory.

The Wolf Fang members were far from weak. But the Bozeses and the guards were just that good. That said, the captain, the two subordinates, and other mercenaries who must've heard what happened were clearly bothered by how greatly they were outperformed.

"What's wrong?" the captain asked when Mitsuha didn't react.

I don't want to say this, but I have to.

"Um, if I'm looking for swordsmen, I'm not going to hire amateurs. There are plenty of expert swordsmen from my country's capital or neighboring territories. I can hire them for a lower wage, too…"

"Oh…"

Considering the exchange rate, it would be much cheaper to hire local mercenaries than to hire the captain and his gang. It'd be nonsensical to pay more money for amateurs.

Trust me, I get it. Being skilled at the sword has a gallantry to it. But there are times in life when I have to make myself clear.

"Your value is that you can use firearm weapons from this world. The moment you pick up a sword, a spear, or a bow, you become an amateur. I can't employ someone like that as a guard."

Oh, shoot. They look absolutely shattered. Well, there's nothing I can do about it. They should bring 12.7 mm anti-materiel rifles next time.

What was that, Captain? Anti-materiel rifles are usually fired from the prone position for extra support from the ground? Firing from the shoulder or hip like normal rifles is really hard? That's a problem…

Well, it's not like firing them by hand is impossible. You can figure it out, Captain.

Huh? You think I'm out of my mind? That's not my problem.

When am I going to take you back to the other world? Call me when you learn to hip-shoot an anti-materiel rifle. Unless it's an emergency, I never intended on taking you to the other world. Especially not for little hunting trips. I only did this time because you begged me to help your depressed subordinates.

Anyway, later.

Mitsuha heard anguished wailing from behind her as she walked away, but she paid it no mind. She had only one response: Not my problem!

Chapter 42:
Gallery Café

It was a few days after the nightmarish monster-hunting trip. Mitsuha had already visited the Bozes's estate to apologize. Iris and Beatrice preyed upon her guilt to play dress-up with her. After that, Alexis yelled at her for not inviting him on the trip. *Cry me a river!*

The mercenary captain spent the last few days studying the viability of explosive warheads on 7.62 mm bullets, but he concluded that packing explosives into such a small warhead wouldn't have much effect. Investing in low-penetrability bullets wasn't worth it. *Not surprising. If that worked, we'd all be using them by now. Don't be hasty, Captain.*

For a nice change of pace, Mitsuha decided to start on her next project: creating a client for her new business, Colette's Sculptures. First, she chose the location: one of the countries she met privately on the night of the Second World-to-World Meeting—W2W2 for short. The country had granted her citizenship, and exempted her from military service and paying taxes.

Mitsuha had already used her influence to work with a real estate agent and secure a location. She'd also put out a job listing, and today was the interview day.

I never thought I'd be conducting job interviews without ever going through the job-hunting process myself... Oh yeah, I did interview people for the maid positions at my county residence now that I think about it. But that was the other world, where the system and standards for hiring are totally different than on Earth. Developed countries on Earth place a lot of value on employee rights, so if I unknowingly hire a crazy person, it won't be easy to fire them.

Mitsuha's job posting went as follows:

Seeking gallery café employees.

One manager/cook. No experience necessary. Living space provided. Salary is $620 per week plus ten percent of the café's net profit.

One waitress. No experience necessary. Salary is $420 per week plus ten percent of the café's net profit.

Five-day work week, social insurance and labor insurance supplied.

Work hours are from 10:00 AM to 6:00 PM. Lunch is covered.

The manager's salary was equivalent to about 300,000 yen a month, and the waitress's would be about 200,000 yen a month, plus commission for both. Mitsuha couldn't give her employees any of the gallery's earnings, but she was willing to offer some of the café's profit as extra motivation. Those salaries would be worth much more in this country than in Japan considering the low cost of living and the lower pay scale, which apparently led her to getting a lot of applicants even though she didn't advertise the posting extensively.

I say "apparently" because the government agency (forgot the name) went through a careful investigation for me during the application phase and eliminated most of the candidates. No foreign spies had slipped into the applicant pool, thankfully, but the agency removed members of criminal organizations and their family and friends, habitual criminals who showed no promise of rehabilitating, corrupt businessmen and their partners who buy out small businesses, and anyone with a suspicious background that could be problematic.

That's way too many shady applicants. And they didn't even know the employer is me. This country's really dangerous!

Huh? You're saying all these people flocked to the application because the job conditions are way too good? And that I should've adjusted the wages to the market instead of just picking a random number that sounded fair to me? Yeah, whoops...

Anyway, it was time to interview the candidates who passed the scary initial screening.

The first interview began in silence as Mitsuha stared at the candidate in confusion.

Who's this kid?

Mitsuha looked over the application multiple times, but the girl hadn't given her age.

"U-Um, Rudina... How old are you?"

"I'm thirteen!"

"Why did you apply to this café?"

"Because there was no age requirement on the application!"

Oh, I forgot to add that... Wait, I've read about something like this! Wasn't there a maid café in Japan that didn't have an age limit, or something like that?

Mitsuha slumped her shoulders.

"...U-Um, should I not have applied?"

Oops, this is a job interview. I have to be professional.

"You circled both the manager and the waitress position on your application. Do you know how to cook?"

"More or less... I'm good at math too."

The rest of the interviews went smoothly. Everyone after Rudina was sixteen or older. Mitsuha wanted a waitress to serve customers, but she didn't care about the gender of the manager. Unfortunately, she had little desire to hire any of the men she interviewed. The government had only eliminated applicants based on their background, not their personality or their ability to do the job, so some completely unqualified people made it to the interview stage.

The men seemed to think Mitsuha was a child, and she got the feeling that a lot of them had ill intentions. When she asked if they had any questions, they would grill her on the whereabouts of her parents, where they lived, and other personal information. *You'd think they were interviewing me!*

They were probably thinking it'd be easy to embezzle money from a rich girl who was using her parents' fortune to start a café for fun, or that they could use her as a stepping stone to get close to her parents. Less of the women seemed to be there for such nefarious purposes. Well, there were some, but she decided to narrow it down to women for the manager anyway. *That makes it easier for me too.*

I could've limited the job listing to women from the beginning, but I didn't want to discriminate based on gender. But if this is how it worked out, fine by me. Keeping the job environment safe for the waitress is part of my duty. I don't wanna have to deal with any workplace harassment.

All right, I'll pick the manager first, Mitsuha thought, going back over the written applications and interview results.

Oh no. Rudina is the most qualified...

There was another important task Mitsuha was working on as she prepared the gallery café.

"Hello. Thank you very much for having me."

"It's an honor! I welcome you on behalf of everyone at this base!"

Mitsuha had been brought to an air base by a middle-aged male diplomat she'd met at W2W2. It was in a different country than her gallery café location. She wanted to avoid relying too heavily on one country; "shallow and spread out" was her motto for diplomatic relations.

The man who was about to give her a VIP tour was the commander of this base.

I'm not sure what his title is. Actually, I'm not even sure if this base belongs to an army, navy, or air force. They all have aircrafts...

The commander brought Mitsuha to his office where he treated her to tea and cakes over a pleasant chat. She decided to accept his hospitality; he was just being polite, as was expected of him, given his position and whatnot.

The tour of the base was to come afterwards. Mitsuha didn't know if he was trying to flaunt his country's power, or if this was a show of political friendship.

I'm so excited! You don't get the opportunity to tour an air base every day! I'm gonna take in as much as I can!

Well, actually, I bet any country would give me a similar tour if I asked.

It became clear during the stroll that this was an air force base.

I doubted this would be an army base given the nature of my request, but there was a possibility it belonged to the navy. Long-distance flights are a navy's trade. I guess the air force would lose face if the navy took this job, though. This mission is a great undertaking for this country—no, for anyone on Earth. Except for the Wolf Fang guys.

The last stop on the tour was the apron next to the runway. This was where they docked the planes so the crew and passengers could get on and off, cargo could be loaded and unloaded, and the aircraft could be refueled. Mitsuha's tour guide led her to one of the crafts. It wasn't a fighter aircraft, but a large passenger aircraft capable of long-distance flight.

An Airbus or a Boeing passenger craft could fly about 8,100 miles, but there was no way she could charter a civilian plane with a whole crew, and she wouldn't be able to keep the mission confidential, either. Which meant that her best bet was to rely on the military. They owned long-range aircraft, maintained confidentiality, and would let her use a plane for free, too.

The base had prepared a tanker aircraft for her. She'd asked for "something that can handle a long haul" and gave them a rough estimate of the cruising range. The tanker craft checked all the boxes.

Well, it's not like it would make much sense to use a giant strategic bomber. A tanker aircraft works. It can refuel itself with its refueling tank, I'm guessing. Seems like common sense to design them that way.

The plane was ready to go. Mitsuha took a moment to use the bathroom and change into a flight suit.

There's a bathroom in the craft too, apparently, and there was no real need to change my clothes, but, you know, airplane toilets aren't exactly pleasant, and who wouldn't want to put on a flight suit while riding a military aircraft? I feel so cool!

Okay, I'm ready. Let's do this!

…Huh? Why's the diplomat coming? And where'd all these other people come from? Oh, they're scholars. Yeah, who'd pass up on such an opportunity…

Well, the more the merrier! All aboard!

Chapter 43:
Reconnaissance

The tanker lifted off and took to the sky.

"We've leveled off," one of the crew members announced. Actually, he wasn't just any crew member; he was an aircraft pilot, here today as her guide.

Let's get going. I don't wanna waste any time or fuel.

"Commencing in thirty seconds," Mitsuha said, and the pilot used the intercom to notify the rest of the crew. She thought it'd be best to warn them ahead of time so the event didn't come as a shock. It was her first time doing something like this, too.

Mitsuha had the air force commander assign lookouts over a swimming pool back at the base until she and the crew returned. In the event of an emergency, she was planning on jumping the entire crew into the water, so she wanted someone there to rescue them.

There was a risk that the crew members could get thrusted onto the ground in awkward positions. A bad landing could break bones. The water would alleviate that. Getting the elevation just right so everyone will land gently on the ground would be difficult if she jumped the whole crew at once, especially in an emergency like the aircraft rapidly spiraling toward the ground. She had to account for

the possibility she could mess up.

I'll never forget the pain from when I appeared slightly above that billiards table and my back and butt crashed into the balls! So yeah, I'd join everyone for a dip in the pool if the situation calls for it.

And that's why I changed into a flight suit! But really, it's because I wanted to try the cool outfit. I'll get someone to take a picture of me later.

Oh, it's time. Here we go!

"I am Nanoha, crosser of dimensions in the name of a wandering god! I cast open a path to another world!" Mitsuha gestured grandly as she chanted in the language of the other world.

I'm a staunch believer in formality. I also want to leave the impression that I need a little time to deliver my world-jumping spell. That could allow me to catch an assailant off guard in the future by jumping away instantly. It's the little things that can save your life down the line.

…Nothing happened. The plane didn't shake or drop like an elevator. *What a letdown.*

The rest of the crew seemed much more excited than Mitsuha, though.

"Whoa, look out the window! We're in a totally different place!"

"S-So this is the other world…"

"Collect a sample of the atmosphere! Now!"

The scholars were scrambling. Mitsuha left them to their business; there was something she needed to do.

She and the pilot looked at each other with a nod, and headed to the cockpit. She left the diplomat behind. The cockpit wasn't that spacious, so he would've only gotten in the way. Mitsuha grabbed a spare ICS headset and a microphone as soon as she entered the cramped compartment. She didn't use the mic on the headset because there was no pedal and it would've been a pain hitting the PTT wall switch every time she spoke.

"Please head for the hills at one o'clock and then straight toward the breakwater at eleven," Mitsuha instructed.

"Roger!"

Mitsuha and the pilot were examining the cardinal directions. They wanted to see if the gyrocompass, which was attuned for Earth, would still be correct even after the world jump. The gyrocompass likely wouldn't recognize if the aircraft was facing a different direction when they jumped worlds. Magnetic orientation might be different too. Even if it was different from Earth's, they could simply adjust the scale mark to match this world's. But it wasn't that simple.

In a world without satellites, they couldn't use GPS navigation. There were no radio stations either, of course, which eliminated LORAN navigation. Their only options were inertial navigation or old-fashioned dead reckoning. They could probably measure their drift, too.

The pilot steered the plane around widely so they could trace a line connecting the hill to the breakwater.

"Standby for the first target... Mark!" the pilot announced at the first mark: the hill.

"Mine says 320 degrees!" Mitsuha read the compass she was holding. "The directional gyro says 312 degrees, and the magnetic compass says 319 degrees!"

Wow, there's almost no measurement error! I did my best not to change the aircraft's direction when I jumped, but I can't believe I was this accurate... Well, I guess I shouldn't be too impressed with myself. The credit goes to the piece of the "thing"—a highly capable body of mental energy that I tore off. That little guy's the one executing whatever I will it. There's no way I could make intricate jumps with vague directions like "take all the recording devices" or "remove a small piece of their swords" on my own. Seems like the extra memory expansion in my brain is helping with the precision work too.

Mitsuha didn't know if this world's magnetic north and true north were a similar distance apart as on Earth, but that hardly mattered. As long as she could use the aircraft's instruments to travel in the direction she wanted, it was good enough.

The plane's current position had a westerly declination of seven degrees. That was the same in Japan... Though there was no point in making a comparison without knowing where this world's true north was.

This world's similarity to Earth supports one of my theories that this isn't a completely different planet, but instead "another Earth" that branched off from the same dimension at some point in history. But is the terrain the same?

Does this world just happen to resemble Earth? Or did something happen to cause a massive number of Earth's organisms—maybe even a whole continent—to world-jump here a long time ago?

Or does evolution simply follow a similar path regardless of worlds?

Is there a race of higher beings that hop across dimensions and plant creatures in different worlds?

I don't know the answer. And I don't really care. Whatever the truth is, it'll have no effect on my life or the lives of anyone else in this world.

"Standby for the second target... Mark!"

Oh shoot, I zoned out!

"Head course 316 degrees!"

"Roger! Head course 316!"

All right, we should be good now. It's not like our destination is a small island. The pilot will probably compensate for any crosswinds. I'll be impressed if we don't find this continent!

The tanker plane was now over the ocean. The scholars had calmed down; they were taking pictures like no tomorrow over the land, but open seas look the same on any planet. There was nothing to document. One person remained glued to a window, probably hoping a water dragon would pop up from the ocean. He might've been a marine biologist.

It'd take a while before they reached the continent Mitsuha was aiming for, so she decided to relax in the back of the craft. There was a chance she'd miss a small island or two on the way, but she didn't want to stand in the cockpit for hours on end. She told the pilot and the others to notify her if they saw anything interesting.

Okay, break time!

Mitsuha ended up falling asleep. The odds of coming across an island while passing straight over the ocean from one continent to another were slim, and sure enough, no one came to wake her up. She took a deep, uninterrupted nap.

Many more boring hours passed.

"I think we should get there soon…" Mitsuha muttered.

She had a general idea of how far away the continent was based on the sea charts she had obtained from the captured ships and what the crew members claimed. Calculating their progress based on the speed of the aircraft, they had to be nearly upon it.

Or so she thought. A few more hours passed until a crew member with an ICS headset in one ear finally announced, "The pilot has spotted land."

The crew already knew they were nearing their destination because of the radar, but now, it was finally in sight. Mitsuha raced to the cockpit.

"Call me Mitsuha Lindbergh! That's the Kingdom of Vanel!"

Well, I don't actually know if we're looking at Vanel or not. It could be a bordering country if we miscalculated our course by a large enough margin.

She put on her headset and instructed, "Continue toward the land. I'm going to study the coastline and see if this is our destination or not."

"Roger that. It is unlikely anyone will see us at this altitude."

Mitsuha agreed. They were too high up for someone on land to hear the roar of the engine. There weren't any anti-aircraft lookouts in this world. If anyone happened to look up, they'd probably just think the plane was a strange bird.

She compared her sea chart to the coastline and confirmed it was indeed Vanel. There was no rush. She had the pilot continue flying over the land for a few hours as she studied the terrain.

As long as Mitsuha had a visual idea of her destination, she was able to world-jump there. Of course, she couldn't remember every single spot after only grazing it once, but she didn't need to. Her highly efficient piece of the "thing" took care of the details. Each location was saved in her memory banks allocated specially for world-jumping. When she jumped, she drew a vague mental picture of the place where she wanted to go and her brain selected a location that applied. *How wonderfully convenient.*

Mitsuha scanned the vicinity as much as she could, so she'd have a workable databank when she needed it.

My ultimate goal here is to learn the state of affairs in Vanel and its surrounding countries, figure out this continent's level of technological advancement, and obtain information about the next research fleet. Obtaining coordinates to jump to is the first step.

The language won't be an issue. And I've already learned a decent amount of the kingdom's details from the captured ships' crew. I even have some Vanel currency, so posing as an ordinary citizen and gathering intel won't be too hard. I'm not gonna do anything crazy like sneak into the royal palace as a phantom thief. Just picking up some rumors off the streets. Nothing dangerous at all.

Getting into the royal palace would probably be a cinch for me, though...

No, don't even think about it!

They continued to fly over the terrain. Mitsuha suspected the pilot wasn't just doing it for her; he probably had orders from his superiors to gather as much information as he could. He kept going even when she told him she had seen enough.

The scholars constantly pestered the pilot to fly lower, but they'd risk being seen by the people below. They'd hear the roar of the engine as well. Mitsuha also wouldn't be able to perceive as wide a range of land at a lower elevation.

Calm down, guys! You have a high-def camera! You may not be able to see much in real time, but you can zoom in on your pictures and study them all you want later!

The pilot finally called it quits when it grew too dark to see. He probably made sure had enough fuel to make it home, but that was hardly necessary with the world-jumper on board.

"Okay, we're going back to the base. We jump in thirty seconds!" Mitsuha performed another strange incantation and jumped the aircraft back to Earth. They appeared a short distance from the air base.

Making the plane appear out of nowhere right next to the airfield would've been stupid. The majority of aviation accidents happen near airfields. I'm sure the base restricted flight of other aircraft today but being extra extra *careful is my motto.*

The pilot safely landed the tanker plane on the runway.

"Thank you for all your help today. It's time I take my leave," said

Mitsuha.

"No need to thank me! It was nothing! Don't hesitate to ask if you need anything else. There are surely other continents you've yet to investigate," the base commander said. The diplomat nodded with enthusiasm.

This probably *was* more than worth it to them, considering the information they obtained and the debt Mitsuha now owed them. But she didn't think there was much value in aerial pictures of a civilization centuries behind Earth. It wasn't like this country could declare war and invade Vanel. They had no way of getting there without her.

For good measure, Mitsuha forbade them from sharing any of the data they obtained with other countries. The scholars' air samples would be useless as well, as Mitsuha's world-jumps automatically left out airborne microbes. The components of the air could be studied, at least.

This country had little to gain from the expedition. Which was exactly why I was okay with planning this mission.

The other world's stage of civilization was already common knowledge to the countries of Earth. Because of that, there wasn't anything this country could learn that Mitsuha didn't want them to. She didn't tell them her real purpose for the flight, either. The story she gave them was that she knew nothing but her own continent and wanted to see a land across the ocean that was mentioned in legend. She claimed, "I estimated the direction and distance to the land based on those legends, although they could be way off."

There's no way she'd spill the beans about her true purpose for seeing the continent: so that she could jump to it. She didn't want anyone finding out how her ability worked.

Oh yeah, I should have the scholars notify me if they spot dragons or anything else dangerous in the zoomed-in pictures. Might come in handy for something.

And on that note, this day trip is done. Now I can pop over to Vanel and do a little investigating whenever I have time. I'll probably stand out a little because the people there look European as well, but there are apparently a few inhabitants from distant lands, so I'm sure it'll be fine!

I can always just flee if things get dangerous. I'm something of an escape artist.

A few days later, Mitsuha received the pictures and the results of the scholars' analysis. When they not-so-discreetly hinted that they wanted a reward, she relented and gave them one of the "Cambrian period-looking" fish caught off the shore of Yamano County. The scholars were ecstatic.

They vehemently refused when Mitsuha offered to teach them how to grill it. *But they're delicious.* When she tried to demonstrate how to prepare it anyway, one of the scholars locked her in a hold from behind to stop her.

Hey, that's sexual harassment, I say! Sexual harass-a-sass, damn it!

Oh, whatever. I guess that was my bad. I may have brought the fish but it's theirs now. I shouldn't have tried to mess around with someone else's stuff. I'll back down.

Mitsuha grabbed the documents they gave her and jumped to the third floor of her general store in Zegleus. *This is top secret stuff… I need to watch out where I open them.*

She sat down and studied the findings. A magnified picture of a port showed dozens of sailing ships large enough to cross the ocean. The vessel sizes were noted in the scholars' analysis.

The images confirmed Mitsuha's suspicion that the ships she captured were older models. Vanel must've been repurposing old ships as research fleets when they deployed a new model. She'd have to see the ships in person to gather more information.

The surrounding countries had similar fleets. Little could be gleaned about their civilization from these pictures alone.

Looks like I'll have to go there myself after all. That was my intention from the start, anyway. Covert small trading between Earth and this world isn't the only way for me to make money. I could also trade between continents in this world. I don't think anyone would mind me operating my business on a slightly larger scale if the trade goods are from the same world.

The exchange rate for gold and silver could be different over there. I could make a killing… No, I should save that as a last resort. It can be my emergency recovery plan: trading gold, silver, and pearl. Gotta trade 'em all!

So this is the New World, Mitsuha thought. *I couldn't stop thinking about it, so I decided to go for a field trip.* She had jumped to a port town in the kingdom of Vanel.

Mitsuha had a rule: a 250-yen allowance cap on travel snacks. She ended up spending 50 yen over the budget, but she ate the extra food before she left the house, so she technically didn't break her rule. She had enough Vanelian currency thanks to the safes on one of the captured ships, as well as the sailors' pocket change which they exchanged for Zegleusian currency.

Oh, the "New World" is what I'm calling this continent, by the way. It's nice and simple.

Night had fallen. Arriving during the day would've been more convenient, but the darkness lowered the chance of someone witnessing Mitsuha appear out of nowhere. Safety first. She could've come during the day by jumping into a forest far from the town where no one would see her, but the trek would've been a hassle. Jumping right outside the town after it got dark was easier and safer.

After doing just that, Mitsuha was now looking for an inn.

Hey, I found one. This'll do.

"Excuse me, do you have a room available?"

It went without saying that Mitsuha looked like a child in this land too, but no business would turn away a customer that paid upfront, be they child or foreigner. It helped that her clothes made her look like a noble or a daughter of a wealthy family.

Mitsuha got a room without difficulty and went right to bed. She had no desire to use the bathrooms here, and the best way to avoid that was by going to sleep immediately. She could always jump back home and take care of her business there if she absolutely had to.

Tomorrow I'll make sure to find a place I can jump to during the day. That'll save me the trouble of jumping here at night and looking for lodging. If I can jump in the morning and leave by dusk, I can make my visits a snappy one-day trip.

Morning came. Mitsuha got up to stretch and loosen up. Her body was stiff from the hard bed. That's when she came to a sudden realization…

Couldn't I have just gotten this room, jumped back home to sleep in my comfortable bed, and returned here in the morning?

Goddamn it! This amazing ability of mine is worthless if I don't have the brains to use it! What other unnecessary pains am I putting myself through? Maybe I should take some time to have a long, hard think about it…

Well, I'll worry about that later. Time to get moving!

The first order of business was choosing a jumping point. After a while of wandering around, she found a heavily wooded area in a park. There was a spot in the middle of the trees that was hidden from view in all directions. While no one would go out of their way to walk into those trees, it wouldn't be too strange to see someone walk out of them. It was perfect.

Next, Mitsuha went to the port to inspect the ships. This was why she chose Vanel's largest port town as her first destination instead of its capital. She didn't bring a camera because she didn't want to draw any attention. All she needed was a good look at the ships' shapes and sizes, their sails, and the number of gun decks. That would give her a decent understanding of their capabilities. The pictures had already given her an idea of what she would find.

Mitsuha finally arrived at the naval port. She couldn't get too close, but she didn't need to. Inspecting the ships from a distance was more than enough.

The ships had two decks and about sixty cannons. They looked similar to a galleon but not as heavily equipped as a ship of the line. The vessels Mitsuha captured were smaller and had fewer cannons. Those really were a generation old… Maybe almost two.

Building ships comparable to Vanel's would be impossible for the Zegleusians. She could provide blueprints of large sailing ships from Earth, but without the foundational skills and knowledge, they'd be too complex for the people of Zegleus to build. While the shipbuilders might've been able to mimic the structure, a tragedy— like leaking, or worse, the keel snapping off—was sure to occur.

That left them with no choice but to make small, fast ships with new long-range cannons to bombard the enemy from a distance. Large-caliber cannons would work too. It wasn't the size of the ship that restricted the caliber of the cannons; the only reason cannons in this era had to be relatively small was because they were muzzleloaders. Those needed to be pulled back inside the ship to reload. Larger caliber cannons would be a viable option if they used the more advanced breechloader design.

Hmm… Vanel's big and slow ships equipped with small-caliber unrifled muzzleloaders that shoot round cannon balls versus Zegleus's medium-sized and fast ships with large-caliber rifled breechloaders that fire cylindro-conoidal bullets…

I like our chances!

"What are you doing here, young lady?" someone asked from behind. Mitsuha was sitting on a tree stump, completely immersed in scouting the enemy fleet.

Ahh! This is the greatest mistake I've made in my life!

Mitsuha used her signature move: Act Like a Child!

"Mommy told me not to talk to strangers…" *It's been a while since I've broken that out…*

"Uhrm…"

Hey, it worked! He's flustered! I can't look older than twelve or thirteen to the people of this land! …Not that I'm happy about it.

The man who approached her was a young soldier, around twenty years old. The insignia on his uniform showed that his rank was this country's equivalent of private first class. Mitsuha had learned the rank insignias from the prisoners.

"Uh, I-I'm not a sketchy person!" the soldier sputtered.

"Mommy said all sketchy people say that."

"Urgh…"

Sweet! He's mega-flustered now! I'd feel bad if I bully him too much, though. He's just doing his job.

"I'm waiting for Daddy to come back. He left on the *Kalliad* so long ago…" The *Kalliad* was one of the three ships she captured in Yamano County.

"Urk..." The soldier choked.

Joining an exploration fleet was a gamble. Not only was there a risk of finding nothing, but there was also no guarantee your ship would even make it home. The possibility of a ship returning couldn't have been very high. And Mitsuha knew for certain the *Kalliad* never would.

But you couldn't tell a young girl there was little to no chance of her father coming home.

"Do you know anything about his ship?" Mitsuha asked.

"Uh, well, I work in a different post, so I don't know much about it. Sorry. Have a good day..." The young soldier took off.

Heck yeah! I won!

The soldier was likely a guard. Mitsuha wasn't inside the base, and it wasn't like the appearance of the ships was a secret. She wasn't doing anything wrong by looking at the ships from here. There were other people watching the ships around her as well. He probably only spoke to her because he was worried about her as a little girl sitting there alone.

Unless... He wasn't hitting on me...was he?

No, don't be ridiculous... I look like I'm twelve or thirteen to these people. No one older than fifteen is gonna make any moves on me.

Suddenly, another voice called from behind. "Hey, are you alone? Wanna get some tea at a café?"

Mitsuha looked up. *Aaaahh! A fifteen-year-old boy is hitting on me! My thoughts became a reality! Behold, the power of the mind!*

He looked like a fresh recruit. His uniform was equivalent to that of a sailor suit on Earth. They weren't identical to Earth's, but they're pretty close. Just like seamen on Earth, sailors here also had to go on long voyages without baths or clean laundry. Their uniforms had a large collar to protect the suit from grime, and to help the wearer hear voices from afar even in strong wind. When you raised the collar up against the back of your head, it made it easier to pick up sound.

The boy also had a scarf around his neck, which could be used as a towel or a handkerchief. The shirt collar was cut into a V shape so it could be torn off if the wearer fell in the water. Swimming with clothes on drained a lot of energy. Regardless of the worlds, form followed function.

Now that Mitsuha thought about it, the age of adulthood in this world was fifteen. Armies tend to recruit young people, so it made sense that fifteen year olds would enlist as military crew here. It wouldn't be surprising if they employed even younger people as child soldiers or recruited them for military youth schools. There were plenty of jobs a child could do, including simple chores, delivering internal messages, lookout, or taking care of an officer's basic needs.

The base probably alternated its soldiers' shifts so there were always people working. It was totally possible that this young soldier was just getting off a night shift or enjoying his day off. And given the time period, Mitsuha figured there weren't any women on base except for a few administrative staff and elderly ladies who ran kiosks... A teenage girl would've been non-existent.

No wonder he's asking me out! Normally I'd reject him out of hand, but my mission here is to learn all I can about Vanel! He could be a valuable, loose-lipped source of information.

A young soldier wouldn't know anything Mitsuha hadn't already heard from the prisoners, but quite some time had passed since they'd left their hometown. Intel from a high-ranking officer was much more valuable than anything a new recruit had to share. But at the same time, being up to date on information was just as valuable. Plus, getting acquainted with a low-ranking soldier before trying to approach an officer was an elementary espionage technique. It was more efficient and reduced the risk of drawing suspicion.

Mitsuha blushed as she looked down. "S-Sure…" she fiddled.

This isn't the first time I've been hit on, you know! I'm perfectly capable of acting in a way that appeals to boys! Hmph!

Admittedly, the one time it happened, I was a high school sophomore, and the boy was in his first year of middle school. I turned him down on the spot! Argh, I was so mad!

I've even been approached by someone a year older than me… She was a girl, though! She said she wanted me to be her petite sœur, *whatever the hell that means! Grrr, I'm getting worked up all over again just thinking about it!*

Mitsuha had to pause and take a deep breath.

Enough of that tangent!

"I know a place that's already open at this time. Let's go!" the boy said hastily. He looked utterly surprised that she agreed. He probably expected her to reject him.

All right. I'm older than him, so let me take the lead here.

"Okay! Sounds good!"

They arrived at a café right by the base and decided to take a table inside. The prices at restaurants in this country differed depending on whether you chose indoor seating or terrace seating. Terrace seating was the most expensive, and the cheapest was at the counter and standing tables. The seated indoor tables were priced in the middle. Terrace seating was almost three times as expensive as the counters.

Mitsuha said she was fine with the counter or the standing tables—she didn't want to make a rookie soldier who had to be younger than her spend too much money—but the boy refused. He clearly wanted to impress her.

The lad would've liked to show off by choosing terrace seats, but there was another problem besides money that stopped him—the café was right next to a large naval base, which meant there was a lot of foot traffic from off-duty soldiers. Some of his colleagues, seniors, and superior officers were among them, and most of them were unmarried or didn't have girlfriends. And the terrace being in plain view of the passersby... *Well, you get the idea.*

"I'll have a coffee," the soldier said when a waiter approached them.

"Can I have a café allongé, please?"

The waiter left with their drink orders, and Mitsuha and the soldier began to chat. He said he wasn't hungry because he ate a free breakfast on his ship. Mitsuha had breakfast at the inn, so she joined him for a drink. Ordering a coffee apparently got you an espresso in this country, so she asked for a café allongé, which was the standard coffee on Earth.

The soldier... *Okay, calling him a "soldier" when he's only fifteen feels weird to me. But he's legally an adult in this world, so I don't want to call him a "boy" either. He looks eighteen or nineteen at most. Calling him a "GI" is too army-ish, and referring to him as a "grunt" sounds demeaning, especially if it turns out he's a non-commissioned officer... I guess sticking with "soldier" is safest.*

Anyway, back to the conversation! I know how to talk to boys, I swear.

"Thank you for inviting me out!" Mitsuha started. "Are you a seaman? Or do you work on land?"

She wanted to learn his position first. That would determine the questions she asked and the credibility of his answers. Boys didn't like admitting to girls that they didn't know something, and he was sure to make something up if she asked him a question he didn't have the answer to. Mitsuha had to determine how trustworthy he was.

"I-I'm a sailor! I work on the *Leviathan*. It's the latest model ship with sixty-four cannons! Isn't that amazing?!"

Bingo! Just what I want!

You could learn a good amount from a ground troop too, but they had to be high enough in rank to handle valuable information. By contrast, even the lowest recruit could tell you a decent amount, including the capabilities of their ship, the weapons on board, and their schedule.

Furthermore, young sailors had a high sense of self-importance. A navy wasn't run by sailors alone; it was also supported by land workers who prepare the ships for navigation. Technically, there was no hierarchy in their positions. But young sailors who embarked on the ships and sailed to battle couldn't help but think of themselves as a big deal, and all it took was a little flattery to loosen their lips.

Based on what Mitsuha learned from the prisoners and her observation of the moored ships, a sixty-four-cannon ship really was cutting-edge. The ships she captured only had forty cannons.

The soldier... *Nope, that's not working for me. I can't get comfortable with the fact that someone this much younger than me can be a soldier. I'll just call him soldier boy!*

The soldier boy probably thought Mitsuha was from a slightly wealthy immigrant family. It was unlikely for him to suspect she was a spy because of how young she looked, and it wouldn't make sense to choose someone who looked like a foreigner for that role. Besides, a spy wouldn't have any business with a low-ranking soldier.

Actually, he probably hasn't thought that far. He's only about fifteen...

It was likely he hadn't thought much about her clothes either. Anyone with a keen eye would notice they were high-quality, but an average teen like him would probably just think she was a commoner girl doing her best to dress up.

Boys have NO IDEA how much girls' clothes cost, and how much time and money we spend on makeup! …Well, I don't personally put much effort into either one. I just used to hear Micchan from the liquor store complain about that all the time.

Anyway, time to start this information war.

Ready… Fight!

"Wow. Such cool." "So sailor. Many fun." Mitsuha tossed in words of affirmation as the soldier boy rambled on and on with breathless excitement.

Good, good. All according to plan.

He was still a kid; in Japan, he would've been in his last year of middle school or his first year of high school. Mitsuha thought he looked college-aged, but that was only because she was Japanese and tended to think foreigners looked older than they really were. He acted much younger than he appeared.

Actually, given the lack of information-sharing technology in this world, his maturity level might be even lower than that.

Wait. There's a microscopic possibility that boys in this world are actually very *matured when it comes to girls due to the lack of activities to entertain oneself with compared to Earth.*

Anyway, while the soldier boy was an adult in this country, he was still a child from Mitsuha's—a Japanese person's—perspective. She, on the other hand, was eighteen, and while she hadn't yet come of age in Japan, she was old enough to read lewd manga or view violent content. Twisting a young boy around her little finger was a cinch for her.

"So, how fast is the sixty-four-cannon ship?" she asked.

"It can go close to fifteen knots with a tailwind! Awesome, right?!"

"Huh? I thought crosswinds gave more speed than tailwinds."

"Whoa, I'm impressed you know that... Yeah, that's true, but most girls have a hard time understanding that, so it's easier to just say tailwind. But yeah, if the sails get a crosswind..."

It sounded like the sailing capability of the newer ships wasn't too different from the captured ones. If the top speed was fourteen to fifteen knots, then the average speed was closer to four or five knots.

He's not actually using knots as the unit of speed, of course. He's using a unit of measurement from this world, and the translator in my brain is converting that into a unit I recognize. One knot is equivalent to one nautical mile per hour, and one nautical mile is about 1.15 regular miles.

The 64-cannon ships aren't as fast as clipper ships like the famous Cutty Sark or the Thermopylae, but they're still pretty impressive. Building ships with vastly superior capability is going to be a tall task. And now that I think about it, sailing is an art that requires years of training to master. Beginners won't stand a chance against the Vanel fleet. This is gonna be harder that I thought...

We'll be at a massive disadvantage in ship size, shipbuilding technology, seamanship, wealth, basic scientific knowledge... Basically in all aspects. Would our ships be able to protect the kingdom when I'm not there?

... There's no way.

If only we could use steam engines... I might as well be wishing upon a star for the ships to shoot laser beams, given our current technology level. *Trying to defeat the enemy ships with ramming attacks would be hard without a motor.*

"Huh? What's wrong, Mitsuha?" The soldier boy looked at her worriedly.

Whoops, I let my gloom show on my face.

"Oh, nothing. I was just comparing your ship to the one that my friend's dad is on... I think my friend said it has forty cannons. I'm worried it's not powerful enough and that it might lose in battle..." Mitsuha said, finding an excuse to talk about the differences between the new ships and the captured ships.

... This boy is a fountain of knowledge. Maybe he's not just a lowly recruit? He could be the son of an officer, or an officer candidate... Or given his age, a junior candidate might be more likely.

"Forty cannons?" he repeated. "That's not weak. Those were our second biggest ships until the new ones were deployed. Plus, a ship rarely sinks in naval warfare. A seaman's life or death is a matter of luck."

Man, he has a mature outlook on life and death for his age... But what he said makes sense. You're gonna have a hard time sinking an enemy ship using simple iron balls without explosives. In this era, victory at sea is achieved by breaking the mast or cutting the ropes to render the ship unworkable, or killing and injuring crew members until the ship is inoperable.

The soldier boy lectured Mitsuha some more. A young boy like him wasn't going to have the conversation skills to impress a girl, and there couldn't be many girls who would gladly talk about ships for this long. That went double for girls who had enough interest and knowledge to ask engaging questions. It was no surprise he was so excited to share everything he knew.

Many cups of coffee later, Mitsuha hinted that it was time for her to go home. It was almost noon.

"Oh, don't say that! I'll treat you to lunch too! I know a really good restaurant!" the soldier boy insisted.

Excellent. He doesn't want to lose a girl who romanticizes sailors and is so knowledgeable about sailing. That works for me—a boy who will tell me anything about Vanel's best ships and its military is an invaluable source of information.

I'll need to keep him on the hook.

Time to use the technique from Micchan's playbook: "How to Knock a Boy's Socks Off" Chapter 3, Clause 2.

Step one: put your fists to your chin and make a cute pose.

Step two: give him a hard jab right in the sweet spot!

"But if I skip lunch, my mom and dad will ground me. Then I wouldn't be able to see you again…"

Nailed it!

"Oh, let me get this one…" Mitsuha stopped the soldier boy who tried to pay for her drinks. Her conscience wouldn't let her sit back and let him pay; she ordered a lot of refills throughout their lengthy conversation. And she had plenty of this kingdom's cash. The crews of the captured Vanelian ships had exchanged their pocket money for local currency, and Mitsuha had claimed what was in their ships' safes.

The soldier boy refused, of course, insisting that it would be ungentlemanly for him to let a girl pay. Mitsuha didn't want to spend the rest of the day racked by guilt, however, so she flustered him with a stern "Are all Vanelian gentlemen so bad at listening to girls?!" and paid before he could utter another word.

Mitsuha had brought small change—silver coins and small silver coins. But she'd used them to pay for the inn, so she didn't have enough of them left to pay for the drinks. *I should've brought small gold coins for change too...* That left her with no choice but to pull a full-sized gold coin out of her pouch. The store employee tried his best to remain calm as he accepted the handsome currency, but the soldier boy was visibly shocked.

Yeah, watching someone pull a gold coin out of a bulging pouch would lead anyone to assume that the pouch is full of them... And in this case, they'd be right.

After they left the café, Mitsuha kept up her "young-lady-from-a-wealthy-family" act and successfully bid him a "hope to see you again" without making any promises. The soldier boy tried to make plans with her, but she evaded him by insisting she didn't know when she'd be free again. He couldn't be too insistent because he didn't know when his next day off would be either. Besides, if his ship departed, he wouldn't be able to see her again for a while.

I know his name and the name of his ship, so if I need to, I can contact him whenever I want. "Soldier boy" is just what I call him in my head; of course I got his real name.

Oh, I should write it down to be safe. Knowing me, I'll forget his name by tomorrow...

Mitsuha left the port, cut across the downtown area, and walked to the opposite side of the town. She was getting lunch as she told the soldier boy, but she needed to go to the other side of town to avoid running into him again.

The goal for the day was to learn as much as she could about Vanel. It was much too early to go home now. The next plan of action was to eat alone at a diner and listen to the customers nearby. That was an important part of gathering information.

The biggest component of intelligence work on an enemy nation was gathering what was available to the public. You then classified that information and analyzed it to determine the nation's intentions. Sending spies to infiltrate the government was a very rare occurrence.

Once she finished lunch, Mitsuha explored the town and shopped while continuing to listen to the people around her. She also gathered what she could by speaking to the store employees and approaching people in parks who looked about her age…which, as you'd expect, meant twelve-year-olds.

It doesn't matter if I run into the soldier boy now that lunch time's over. I can just tell him I snuck out of the house again after eating with my family.

And so, Mitsuha went on intel-gathering a few more times, once every couple of days, bringing season one of Mitsuha's Vanel Reconnaissance—the Naval Port Arc—to an end.

For the next few days, Mitsuha jumped around between her county, her general store in the capital, the gallery café she was preparing on Earth, and her house in Japan. Once she caught up on her responsibilities, she resumed her spy work in the New World.

She didn't go to the port town this time. She chose it as her first stop partially because she wanted to learn all she could about the ships, but there was another major motivation: she wanted to gain familiarity with the country before she went to her ultimate destination. Asking overly ignorant questions carried the risk of drawing suspicion to herself.

But now that Mitsuha had the minimum knowledge a foreigner visiting Vanel should know, she was ready for her main stop. She had already picked out a jumping point. By comparing a map of the port town with the aerial photographs and referring to her memory of the reconnaissance flight, she knew she could manage.

I'm gonna have to go after dark like last time, unfortunately, but it shouldn't be an issue. Time to set out!

My destination: the capital of Vanel. My objective: gather information and secure a base of operations.

Operation Viscount of Monte Yamano begins now!

Chapter 44:
The Viscount of Monte Yamano

"I'd like to open an account..."

Mitsuha was visiting a bank.

"Oh, uh, yes. Right this way, please." The receptionist led her to a private room.

This Vanelian bank differed greatly from the banks in Japan. It wasn't crowded enough to necessitate a line or hand out numbered tickets. Creating a bankbook wasn't nearly as simple as writing your name and address on a piece of paper and showing your identification. A child of a peasant couldn't possibly open an account. But the receptionist could easily tell by looking at Mitsuha's attire that she wasn't here as a prank.

Holy heck, these bags are heavy. Mitsuha set down the two shoulder bags she was lugging onto the table. *Why did I do that to myself...?*

"I want to open an account, convert these into money, and deposit it," she said as she unzipped her luggage.

There were about thirty pounds of 98% pure gold ingots in each bag. About sixty pounds of gold would net a little over one hundred million yen in Japan, but going by Vanel's rate, they'd be worth just under four hundred million yen.

"I brought this gold hoping it will be enough to cover my living expenses while I'm here," Mitsuha explained. "I don't have any of this country's currency, so I was wondering if you could convert them and put it in an account for me..."

The receptionist widened her eyes and stood frozen. After about ten whole seconds, she stammered, "P-P-Please wait a moment!" and darted out of the room. She was probably calling someone above her to handle this.

I actually borrowed all this gold. I asked the king to lend it to me for the sake of the kingdom—nay, the continent—no questions asked, and he actually did it. He isn't even going to charge interest. What a generous guy...

The receptionist returned with two middle-aged men. She returned to her own duty, leaving Mitsuha in the room with the two men. *Hmm, neither of them is the fine and rugged kind of middle-aged.*

"Thank you very much for choosing our establishment, miss! I am Morley, the president of this bank, and he is Agress, the vice president," one of them greeted.

Wow, they're the top two people in the company. Let's not waste any time...

"I am Viscountess Mitsuha von Yamano. I'm here visiting from another country. It's nice to meet you." She disclosed that she was a foreign noble who was planning to stay in Vanel for a little while, that she brought gold ingots for her spending money because they'd be easier to convert than her country's currency, and that she wanted to open a small shop to advertise goods from her land—mostly just for fun. "Can you please convert these gold ingots into this country's currency?"

"Gladly!" the men harmonized. They were probably excited

about the handling fee they were going to charge her.

"Would it also be possible to introduce me to a trustworthy real estate agent?"

"Yes ma'am!" they responded in sync again.

Is there any point in them both being here if they're gonna say the same thing?

Mitsuha gave the bankers the name of the inn she was staying at and left. Bluffing to that extent at the largest bank in the capital was going to give her quite the reputation.

Four hundred million yen's worth of gold probably wasn't that much money to the president of a major bank. But what if it was brought in as "a little spending money" for a young daughter of a foreign noble to play with? That changed everything. It implied that her parents gave her this gold as an allowance and let her carry it around without guards, and that sixty pounds of gold ingots was so insignificant to them that they weren't worried about the possibility of it being stolen.

The bank president and his employees had to be wondering just how rich her parents were. Mitsuha's peerage likely also led them to assume that her parents were high-ranking nobles with multiple peerages in the family, and that they doted enough on their daughter to give her one.

That conjecture led them to a natural conclusion—that there were hundreds, maybe even thousands of times more wealth where those ingots came from. In the bank president's eyes, Mitsuha wasn't just a girl with four hundred million yen worth of gold, she was the daughter of a noble family with a fortune worth hundreds of billions of yen.

Mitsuha hadn't said a word to imply any of that. All she did was mention her peerage. That said, she knew how it would sound.

No one would assume she inherited her title from deceased parents; someone like that wouldn't have the time or freedom to go on a casual romp to a foreign country.

I only spoke the truth. It's their fault for coming to the wrong conclusion.

Mitsuha headed to the bank the next day to be introduced to the real estate agent. This time to rent. She wanted to get done with the chore of finding a building with a living space to set up her shop and establish a point she could safely jump to at any time.

The reason she was renting instead of buying was because she didn't need any main bases in this world beyond Mitsuha's General Store in the capital and her Yamano County residence. She planned to abandon her Vanelian base if necessary, so buying it would be silly. Purchasing without a backer also felt like a lot of work; she'd probably have to fill out paperwork and provide a personal reference, which would just be a hassle.

The real estate agent was unlikely to sweat the details if she paid upfront for a rental. The bank would probably vouch for her.

I'm sure it's all gonna work out!

The bank president rushed to Mitsuha as soon as she entered the building. He'd probably been waiting for her since the bank opened.

"Is the real estate agent here?" Mitsuha asked.

"Yes, of course. He is waiting for you. I'll bring him right here."

Man, this takes me back to when I met Lutz to shop for a storefront.

"Thank you for coming. I'm Zaunal, the real estate agent. The bank president has informed me what you are looking for, so I picked out several properties for you."

The real estate agent worked fast. You had to be good to be chosen by the president of the largest bank in the capital. He'd already prepared a list of properties that matched the demands Mitsuha relayed to the bank president: a small shop available for rent with a living space attached.

Mitsuha didn't intend to renovate the building this time. She couldn't do much as a renter, and it wasn't like she was planning on living there twenty-four seven. She could just jump home whenever she had to relieve herself or take a bath.

If the attendees of the World-to-World Meeting heard that I jumped back to Earth every time I had to use the bathroom, they'd grab me by the collar and shake me, Mitsuha chuckled to herself.

After whittling down the options and inspecting the properties in person, Mitsuha rented a small two-story building. The first floor was constructed as a storefront, an office, a small storage space, and a bathroom—which she didn't plan to use. The second floor had a living quarter she also didn't intend to use.

I'm only renting this place to create the illusion that I live here and to secure a safe jumping point. The building I chose is pretty decent—I'm presenting myself as rich, so it wouldn't make sense if I rented some shoddy property; I have to keep up appearances. One of the biggest reasons I chose this building is because it's located in the middle of the city's aristocratic district. It also neighbors the local guard station. Which felt like a necessity given that the shop is going to be carrying expensive goods and be run solely by a little girl. That's an enticing combo for robbers, but no one would be dumb enough to try breaking in with a guard station next door. I'm essentially getting free security guards. I won't have to worry about leaving the building unattended.

That was probably why the bank president and Zaunal chose this building as the first candidate. Mitsuha appreciated their consideration.

There was no need for any interior renovation this time. The building was originally used as a shop, and there were iron bars set into the windows for security. She was going to buy the display cases and other furnishings in Japan.

Unlike Mitsuha's General Store, the purpose of this shop wasn't to make money, it was to draw attention to herself. She wanted to display her technological prowess enough to attract people who sensed an opportunity to make money, but not enough to invite suspicion. She would have to be careful not to sell anything that might inspire Vanel's people with technological improvements. Her store would carry items that looked luxurious but weren't necessarily new inventions as well as unusual items with a foreign flair.

Profit was not the goal here. The shop would be a simple tool to help Mitsuha grow her name and build connections; a stepping stone to enter high society, gather information, and become an influential figure. She also hoped people would sell her samples of tools and machinery she could use to improve technology in Zegleus. Earth technology was too advanced for the people of Zegleus to understand and learn from, and the exchange rate rendered items from Earth too expensive.

Mitsuha had noticed that Vanelian gold coins were lower quality than their Zegleusian counterparts. They were slightly larger yet weighed about the same. That meant the gold content was lower, making the metal a little less valuable. She couldn't quite tell just by looking at the coins and touching them, so she had them tested.

Despite that, Mitsuha got the sense that one gold coin was worth more than 100,000 yen to the people of Vanel, which was slightly more valuable than Zegleus's. She didn't know if gold was simply worth more here, or if people just trusted their kingdom to back the value of its currency. Zegleus—the Old World—didn't have the same level of credibility, so a coin's only value was the metal it contained.

It seems like I'd be better off collecting solid gold and actual products than Vanelian gold coins. The former I can sell in our kingdom.

Mitsuha was only going to use Vanelian currency here; she didn't want to put gold and silver coins from Zegleus into circulation in an enemy country. The plan was to recoup the initial investment of sixty pounds of gold and pay the king back.

All right, time to start working on my new shop, Yamano Commodities!

What if we just jacked Vanel's best ships?

Such a naive idea did occupy Mitsuha's brain once. Not the shipbuilding techniques, but the ships themselves. She could just pop over to a Vanelian harbor, steal a completed and fully equipped ship, and jump it back to Bozes County while leaving the crew behind. There was nothing stopping her from taking an entire fleet, even.

That would give Zegleus a full fleet without anyone needing to break a sweat. They'd never have to worry about the arrival of another research fleet from Vanel or another country from the New World or beyond ever again.

But if the kingdom relied on that method, how would it fare if Mitsuha disappeared? Would the people be able to learn how to build ships just by making an imitation of the ones they already had? Technology shouldn't be taken so lightly. If you introduced Japan to Yamato-class battleships at the beginning of the Meiji era, there was no way the country would be able to replicate them right away. The people would be more excited to try out their new toys than they'd be to study its engineering.

Thus, Mitsuha rejected that idea. Zegleus wouldn't have a future unless it built its own ships. Besides, the Vanelian navy would recognize their stolen ships immediately if they saw them. Peace would be impossible after that.

But there was no way Zegleus's shipbuilding technology could rival Vanel's. What, then, could they do?

The only answer was to win with weapons. They could use small ships and equip them with a small number of disproportionately large guns. They'd be monitor vessels, essentially. They'd fire from outside of the enemy's range.

What's that? Matsushima-class cruisers failed? Yeah, they did. They weren't effective in battle. Their mistake was equipping such a small ship with one large-caliber gun. The rapid-fire guns that were only meant to be secondary armaments did most of the work. But what if we shrink the size of the gun and use explosive cylindro-conoidal bullets...? Or we could just forget about battling on the open sea, and instead specialize the ships to be rowed like galleys and intercept the enemy on the coast.

Hmm, I'll need to consult with the king...

Mitsuha bought display stands and cases in Japan, and jumped them to Yamano Commodities in Vanel. She couldn't write them off as a business expense for Colette's Sculptures because she wasn't going to use them in Japan.

She used her world-jumping ability to position the display stands and cases in the shop. That was a much easier way of moving heavy objects than dragging them across the floor. *What a mundane use of my ability...*

Next, she added curtains and light fixtures from Japan that looked fancy but weren't actually expensive, then finished setting up the shop with similarly luxurious-looking decorations. *Now I just gotta line the shelves with products!*

Mitsuha was invited to a party. She didn't know the host, but the bank manager told him about her, so she was sure he was a credible man. She'd mentioned to the bank manager that she wanted to network with the local high society but didn't know where to start. He went ahead and made the arrangements.

The man who sent the invitation was a count, and the party was for his daughter's birthday. Unlike in Zegleus, Vanelian nobles threw elaborate birthday parties for their children even before they reached adulthood. Made sense, though, given how nobles got engaged before their coming of age. That said, the only social functions children were allowed to attend were birthday parties for unmarried nobles.

I still look like a child, so this is the perfect event to invite me to. Actually, wait. My peerage means I'll be treated as the head of a noble family. The heads of noble families can attend any party they want, even if they're underage.

...I'm an adult though! I turned fifteen a long time ago, damn it!

Anyway, I was probably invited because the bank president convinced the count he has something to gain from meeting me. But that's too bad! The bank president just assumed that on his own!

Mitsuha put on the dress she wore when she was appointed as a viscountess and headed out. She chartered a private carriage to get there. It was hardly appropriate to walk or take a horse-drawn cab.

A sea of eyes turned toward her when she entered the party venue. *Just how many people did the bank president tell about me... Well, the first order of business is greeting the host: the count and his family.*

"Thank you very much for inviting me," Mitsuha said.

The count's family consisted of him and his wife, a girl who looked around eighteen, two boys who looked around sixteen, and a girl who looked around thirteen. The birthday party was for the count's second daughter, which meant it was for the youngest child.

"Th-Thank you for coming. Please, be at ease and enjoy yourself. I will introduce you to everyone later." The count sounded a little shaken. He, his wife, and his oldest daughter were staring at Mitsuha's chest.

Not in a pitiful kind of way! My chest isn't so miserable it would shock someone silent at first glance! Urgh... I need to make sure they don't find out my real age... I especially can't have them knowing I'm older than their youngest daughter!

Their eyes weren't on her chest, but on the pearl necklace she was wearing. She bought this one for 6,200 dollars, much cheaper than the 1.3-million-yen necklace she sold to Lady Iris.

Mitsuha purchased this one abroad. Buying it in Japan would've necessitated using Colette's Sculptures to make a deal and recoup the cost, after which she would lose a hefty amount of money from the exchange rate and handling fees, to say nothing of her worst enemy—taxes. It was much simpler to buy one abroad with dollars.

This necklace was only worth about half as much as the last one, but Mitsuha hadn't heard anything about successful pearl farming on this continent either. It should still be pretty valuable despite the lower quality.

Okay, time to start the mission!

Mitsuha faced the youngest daughter and smiled.

"Happy birthday! I brought a present for you!" she said, taking off her necklace and putting it around the girl's neck. *This is the same method I used with the second daughter of the Pasteur family after I missed her debutante ball. Nothing like the reassurance of using battle-tested strategies!*

Crash! Shatter!

The sounds of glasses and tableware breaking here and there

sprang across the venue.

Geez, there's a lot of clumsy people in here, Mitsuha thought.

The youngest daughter was gaping, speechless. The count was supporting his wife, who looked like she was about to collapse, and the two boys were doing their best to hold up the oldest daughter.

…Huh? Did I go overboard with the value again? But this one's only worth half the 1.3-million-yen necklace. The first one is one of the highest-valued in this world, so I didn't think this one would be too shocking…

"Wh-Wh-Wha…" The count was going pale.

Aren't people's faces supposed to go red at times like this?

"W-We cannot accept something of this value…"

Huh? But going by their sense of money, this necklace is only worth about 7 gold coins for people here. If you were to actually convert the cost of the necklace into their currency it would be 28 gold coins, but that's just the simple exchange rate. Given the value of gold coins in this society, 7 gold coins would be accurate. That's, like, two or three months of a commoner's income. And for a noble, a month's worth of a child's allowance.

Just how much are pearl necklaces worth in a world without pearl farming…

"Um, I just wanted to give this to you to show my appreciation for being the first in this country to invite me to a party, and to commemorate making my first friend in this land… Or do you not want to be friends with a foreigner like me…" Mitsuha hung her head dejectedly. The youngest daughter quickly shook her head.

Sweet! I made a friend! Mitsuha thought. *Oh, my neckline—or my chest, I guess—looks empty without the necklace. That wouldn't be a problem for most women, but it doesn't look great when I wear a simple dress without an accessory around my décolleté. It looks, you know, a little meager, or…totally flat… Don't make me say it!*

It was for that reason that Mitsuha prepared a spare accessory. She fished it out of a side pocket on her dress and put it on. Adorning her chest this time was a vibrant red gemstone. It was a necklace with a Burmese pigeon blood ruby, the highest quality ruby there was. The stone weighed five carats, and had no inclusions or scratches, making it totally translucent. The ruby alone was worth well more than one million yen. Imagine what the value would be if it was made into jewelry by adding a gold or platinum frame or diamonds as accent stones.

That is, if it was a real stone. It's an artificial ruby, of course.

Being artificial didn't make it fake—it still was a genuine ruby. It just happened to be made by humans with science. The stones' components and molecular structure were the same as natural rubies. The only differences compared to a natural ruby were that there were almost no inclusions—or impurities—and the color was a uniform, pretty shade of red.

It was just like how you could identify fake Louis Vuitton bags because they were sturdier and better sewn than the real ones. Some artificial rubies were intentionally given impurities and scratches to make them appear more authentic, because no matter how similar the manmade versions were, real rubies were worth significantly more.

Flux-grown rubies were a little expensive, and those made with the flame fusion method were essentially worth nothing. Some artificial rubies were disguised so well that even experts—including those who were knowledgeable of how artificial rubies were made—had trouble identifying them.

In a world without artificial rubies that is centuries behind scientifically, it would never occur to anyone that this isn't natural. The lack of inclusions and total smoothness are usual giveaways for artificial rubies, but to these people, the ruby around my neck looks valuable beyond belief.

The party hall was dead silent. That was perfectly understandable. Mitsuha had a pearl necklace not even a king would possess. And she'd just given it away to a stranger without a second thought—as casually as giving a friend a hand-knitted scarf.

No one would do such a thing unless they were an idiot or stupidly rich. And to the eyes of the rest of the nobles in this room, this girl did not look like an idiot.

Despite the fact that she was, indeed, a considerable idiot.

Mitsuha had been told that the 1.3-million-yen necklace possessed unimaginable value in this world, so she assumed that a necklace half its value would be seen as a perfectly ordinary necklace. A little on the nice side, perhaps, but nothing shocking.

But therein lied the flaw in her reasoning. A bomb that packed half the force of a hydrogen bomb was hardly an average explosive. Similarly, while the 700,000-yen pearl necklace wasn't as valuable as the first, it still defied all logic for the people of this world.

On top of that, there was the spare necklace set with the most flawless ruby anyone in the room had ever seen. A *spare*. A huge hunk of the finest ruby was carelessly stashed in her pocket as a mere backup.

All eyes in the room once again focused on Mitsuha's chest. No one said a word.

This is really embarrassing! She turned to the count's family and tackled the awkward situation with the only method she knew: cracking a joke.

"Please, stop staring at my chest! You're making me blush!"

Surely that'll win a few giggles. However…

"Huh? Your chest?" The count and his entire family were dumbstruck. Their eyes darted away with expressions that looked like something between condolence and sorrow.

"Don't look at me with pity! Laugh at my joke!"

A little girl behind Mitsuha muttered, "You may not have a chest, but at least you have enough treasures to fill one…"

"Pfft…"

"Heheh…"

"Ahahaha!"

A few people in the room burst out laughing, unable to contain themselves.

"Wow!" *I'm saved! This girl rescued me from that awkward situation!* Mitsuha turned around with moist eyes and grabbed the hands of the girl who lightened the mood. "Thank you! Thank you so much!"

"Uh…"

The girl, who was around twelve or thirteen, looked stupefied.

"My name is Micheline de Mitchell…" the girl said.

"Cool. I'm gonna call you Micchan!"

"Whaaat?!"

The girl who came to the rescue turned out to be the daughter of a marquis. She went out of her way to help Mitsuha by telling a dirty joke, which probably went against the refined noble etiquette she was taught.

I need to repay the favor! One sip of water in the desert is worth more than a hundred fine bottles of wine bought in a city. By that logic, I suppose this will do.

"Let me offer you this as thanks," Mitsuha placed her ruby necklace around Micchan's neck.

"HUUUH?!" the guests gasped.

Mitsuha then pulled a five-carat emerald necklace out of her pocket and put that on herself. This one was also artificial—the gold and silver frame and chain were worth more than the rock.

…That was my last one. I like to be prepared, but not even I would bring three spares.

"WHAT THE HELL?!" The entire ballroom rumbled in astonishment.

Whoa guys, keep your voices down. That's improper language to use at a noble party… Mitsuha thought. *Anyway, this party is for the count's second daughter. A newcomer like me shouldn't hog the spotlight for too long.*

She grabbed Micchan's hand and led her across the room.

"Thanks for earlier, Micchan!"

"You're sticking to that weird nickname, aren't you…" she sighed in exasperation.

If something's bothering you, feel free to tell me! I'd be happy to help, Micchan!

After talking to her for a little bit, it became clear that Micchan didn't have many friends.

"I-It's not like people *don't* want to be my friend! It's just that there aren't many girls my age in other marquis families. When I do talk to girls my age, it causes, um…weird factions to form… And talking to boys isn't any better either. It starts conflicts among families, which then leads to rumors of engagement. Some boys will even start those rumors themselves…"

"Yikes…"

I guess that can't be avoided when you're a marquis's daughter and as cute as her. Her slightly standoffish personality is sure to make any boy want to chase her.

So yeah, like all nobles, Micchan is a cutie. Men in power only marry beautiful women, so it makes sense that all their kids are attractive. Nobles are like the thoroughbreds of society. Hate the race, not the horses.

"Well, you have nothing to worry about with me!" Mitsuha assured her.

"Huh?"

"I'm a foreign noble, so I'm not a part of any faction. That makes me a lone wolf. There's nothing wrong with us being friends!"

Micchan froze and stared speechless.

A marquis's family was sure to have influence in the world of politics. There was also a chance it produced a lot of high-ranking soldiers. *I don't feel good about taking advantage of a friend, but she's a very enticing source of information. I can't let her get away!*

"Are you…"

Huh? I didn't catch that last part, Micchan.

"Are you *stupid*?! Do you really think a girl who hands out national treasure-level necklaces like candy could possibly be free of factions? Every faction in high society is going to fight over you! You're going to be at the center of a massive storm! You'll cause more trouble than I *ever* could!"

What… I wanted to gain influence in high society and use my connections to tour their military facilities and ask about politics, but… Did I mess up again?

Mitsuha looked around and saw that everyone at the party— including the host family—was looking at her and Micchan and listening to their conversation…with a ferocious glint in their eyes.

"…Yeah," Mitsuha said.

"Huh? I beg your pardon?"

"I'm answering your last question. You asked if I'm stupid…

117

And I think I am. I'm a real dummy…"

Mitsuha drooped her shoulders. Micchan let out a dramatic sigh at her new friend.

"Ladies and gentlemen," the count announced, "it is my pleasure to introduce Viscountess Mitsuha von Yamano, a noble from a distant land who's making her debut in Vanelian high society today! Viscountess Yamano, please come over here!"

Wow, that was impressive, Mitsuha thought. *A host needs to know how to command the crowd in any scenario. If he doesn't undo the damage I've done, his daughter's birthday party will be ruined. Micchan and I are eating up way too much attention. This is an important party to find a potential fiancé for his daughter, and she's being totally brushed aside… I'm sure he wants to get my introduction out of the way to get the party back on track.*

Mitsuha headed to where the count was so she could help him move the party along.

"Here she is, Viscountess Mitsuha von Yamano, the young noble lady from a distant land who already possesses her own peerage. As you've seen, she is close enough with my daughter to give her this valuable necklace, and the two of them along with Marquis Mitchell's daughter have developed a special friendship…"

Wait! Hold the freakin' phone! When the heck did that faction form?!

Oh, Micchan's shrugging like she's so done with me. I see, so this is what she wanted to avoid…

I'm so sorry! I'll make up for it, I swear!

"I've been told that Viscountess Yamano came to our country to broaden her horizons. She aspires to share goods from her home country and deepen our cultural exchange. She opened a shop in the center of the city for this purpose."

The gleam in the guests' eyes intensified. They were probably imagining that her collection of "goods" would include more pearls and gems or other items they could use to turn a profit. Mitsuha was handing out luxurious accessories so freely, anyone would assume her country was a major gemstone-producing nation and was selling them for cheap.

"Now, Viscountess Yamano, would you please give a word of greeting?"

Whoa, don't put a girl on the spot like that! I guess I can't get away with not speaking here, though. Whatever. Time to wing it...

"Greetings, everyone. Thank you, Count, for your kind introduction. I am Viscountess Mitsuha von Yamano. I'm from a faraway country I doubt many of you have heard of. I'd love to talk more about my homeland if we have the chance.

"Thank you for inviting me to my first party in Vanel. I look forward to getting to know all of you," Mitsuha gave the most minimal self-introduction she could manage. She didn't mention her country and succeeded in confusing everyone even further.

Well done, me! Now to spend the rest of the party selecting people who have value to me and mingle with them.

Or at least, that was her goal as she bowed and tried to return to Micchan. She was stopped in her tracks by a crowd of nobles who were climbing on top of each other to talk to her.

"I am Viscount Segoll. I'd love to form a friendship with you as two nobles who share the same rank—"

"Hello, I'm Count Ralt. It would be an honor to have a beautiful young lady from abroad like you over to my estate so we can exchange ideas—"

"I'm Count Beenvict. Would you be willing to discuss establishing trade with my family?"

One after another, they came at her. It was never ending.

Who am I, Prince Shotoku?!

"I'm Marquis Mitchell. It seems I owe you for the kindness you showed my daughter…" A man stepped in.

…Is he Micchan's father? Whoa, that smile is not reaching his eyes! Is he mad because I roped his daughter into some weird faction? This is bad! Mitsuha panicked. She looked up at him—he was much taller than her—and uttered without thinking:

"A-Are you buwwying me?"

Waah, what did I just say?! And why'd I have to go that way?

Micchan's father stared with an expression Mitsuha wasn't sure how to describe. It was somewhere between stunned, dumbfounded, and aghast. The people around them had stiffened and gone silent as well.

How can I fix this…

Ten seconds passed before sound finally returned to the world.

Ten seconds may sound like nothing, but I'm telling you, ten seconds in that kind of situation feels really long! An eternity of awkwardness!

Anyway, Micchan's father has rebooted.

"No, I'm not bullying you, but…"

Why'd you have to say that?! Everyone finally thawed, and you just froze them up again!

Mitsuha's conversation with Micchan's father resumed once everyone returned to their senses. They were all listening to them for some reason. Nobody else in the room was talking.

"I'm sorry, Micchan. I didn't mean to put you in a difficult position…" Mitsuha apologized.

"Micchan? Are you talking to Micheline, or…?"

Wait, did I just call him Micchan too? Oh yeah, that nickname could work for him because of his surname—no, Mitsuha! Hold it in!

Don't you dare start laughing!

But I just called this stern, bearded man "Micchan" as if he was a cutesy little girl…

Nooooo, stop!

"Pfft… Bahaha, ahahaha!" Mitsuha burst out laughing.

I can't! I just can't!

Micchan's father looked at Mitsuha blankly as she laughed, then once he inferred her train of thought, his face went red and he started laughing too. "Bahahaha!"

A very unladylike laugh burst out next to me. "Ahahaha! What a silly thing…to call him… Ahahaha!"

Micchan, too, had realized why Mitsuha was laughing. Two people in the whole room understood her.

We have a similar sense of humor. Not sure how I should feel about that…

Once the three of them finally caught their breath, they moved to the corner of the room to chat.

"Phew, I haven't laughed that hard in a while. I thought I was going to pass out… And I don't know how long it's been since I've seen Micheline laugh like that…" Marquis Mitchell seemed overjoyed to see his daughter's bright smile.

Is it okay for a marquis's daughter to belly-laugh like that in front of a crowd of nobles? Wouldn't it be more appropriate for her to cover her mouth with a fan and go, "ohohoho"?

Oh, wait. I'm a noble too! And a viscount to boot!

Ah, whatever. Better not to think about it.

Marquis Mitchell was keeping Mitsuha to himself at the moment. There was no one above him in rank at the party. The host of the party was a count, and therefore below him. The bank president couldn't easily reach out to people of higher rank, so a count's party was the best he could offer Mitsuha. The marquis apparently only came because it was a birthday party for a girl close to his daughter's age, and he wanted to give her an opportunity to make a friend because he was worried about her. Micchan didn't want to, but he practically forced her to come along.

It wasn't just the marquis's presence that was preventing anyone from approaching Mitsuha; the presence of Micchan also steered people away. Wedging oneself between two children who were forming a friendship was something that went against the good sense of any adult, let alone a noble.

But the nobles' patience was wearing thin. Before long, they started loading up and firing child missiles their way.

"Greetings, Viscountess Yamano…"

Here they come…

Mitsuha didn't know if these children were from counts' families or barons' families, but none of them had peerage. By contrast, Mitsuha had claimed herself to be a viscount, which led everyone to believe that her parents must be counts or above. The adults in the room were probably wondering if she received her rank because she was the heir to her parents' house, or because they'd given her their second or third peerage.

Their misunderstanding came from the fact that Mitsuha hadn't shared anything about herself. The nobles figured she didn't want to, and they all knew better than to pry. They also seemed to find her reluctance to talk about her home heartwarming out of the assumption that she wanted to make her own way in this land rather than rely on her parents' influence. Mitsuha was happy to go along with that misunderstanding.

These people don't even know if women are allowed to inherit peer-

age in my kingdom… Well, they technically are, but only when there are no male children or if the male heirs get disowned.

Oh, I just realized I naturally started calling Zegleus "my kingdom." I don't even use the name that often. I guess I consider it my homeland just as much as I do Japan, at this point. Not because I was given peerage—but because so many people who are important to me live there. I truly care about Zegleus.

Then what about this country? I've met so many nice people, including the friendly soldier boy, the bank president, Micchan, Micchan's father, and more…

"Enemies," huh…

Our kingdom has technically declared war on Vanel, not that the people here know that. But if the two nations can avoid an all-out war, there's a chance we could form an amicable relationship.

…I wouldn't give that the best odds, unfortunately. The nobles, politicians, and merchants of this land are unlikely to see our continent as anything other than a massive treasure trove of land to conquer, riches to acquire, and possibly people to enslave. They won't treat us as equals. Military officers won't give up a perfect chance for fame and glory, either. They'd definitely advise invasion.

We have no choice but to prepare for an attack and buy ourselves time by delaying their discovery of our kingdom—no, our whole continent—for as long as possible. It sucks, but that's reality…

"Hello, Lady Mitsuha and Lady Micheline. I'm Amia, the daughter of Count Elliburg!"

"I'm Jerram. I'm from a baron's family…"

The child missiles struck one after another. Marquis Mitchell quietly slipped away, not wanting to impose on the children as they made friends. Micchan tried to do the same—she really seemed to struggle around people—but Mitsuha grabbed her arm.

I'm not letting you escape!

There was no end in sight as Mitsuha was subjected to one conversation after another with the young guests.

Every child followed the exact same pattern—they would give Mitsuha a compliment, ask a question with the purpose of squeezing a little information out of her, and then say something to puff up their own family. Their parents had instructed all of them to get close to Mitsuha, and they all glanced at the adornment around her neck as they spoke.

They're just kids—they shouldn't be playing politics! I'd much rather get back to trying to wheedle information out of the adults, Mitsuha thought. She tried to escape using Micchan as a decoy.

But she didn't get anywhere; Micchan was vice gripping her arm. The anger in her eyes was very clearly saying, "I'm *not* going to let you leave me behind!"

Yeah, that's fair…

And so Mitsuha suffered for a while longer…

Micchan shares the same nickname as my childhood friend from the liquor store. I ended up calling her that without thinking because her first and last name both start with "Mi," and meeting her reminded me a little of when I met the original Micchan in kindergarten.

I doubt I'll ever have much chance to see the original Micchan again, and this Micchan will never go to Japan. Some part of me might've wanted to relive the good old days by giving the nickname to this girl. I feel a little bad for the Japanese Micchan, though…

Anyway, it's about time I shake these kids. I didn't come to this party to make friends with a bunch of kids.

Mitsuha turned to the children. "My apologies, but there are some duties I must perform as Viscountess Yamano…"

There was no way the children could detain her after hearing that. If these children were old enough to attend a birthday party hosted by another family, then they should know that parties were an important place of work for nobles with peerage.

Mitsuha escaped the ring of kids, and Micchan followed behind her. That was expected—if she didn't take that chance to escape, she would've been barraged by the them all on her own.

Micchan hurried toward her parents, and Mitsuha was immediately swarmed by nobles.

"Viscountess Yamano, would you be willing to talk about your country?"

"I would love to hear about it as well. Sharing knowledge of our lands could help us all in the future!"

I haven't said a word about my origin yet, so I'm not surprised they're curious.

The nobles didn't know where she was from. Was it a wealthy nation, or was it just her family that was wealthy? Did her country mass produce gemstones, or were they bought with money made through other means? They wouldn't get any answers until they figured out where her homeland was.

The nobles likely assumed her country was on this continent, and relatively close. Mitsuha spoke their language fluently, after all, and she couldn't have traveled far without any family or attendants to accompany her. She didn't look like the people around here, but there were a few ways to explain that, such as her father marrying a foreign noble or royal for political reasons, or taking a woman from a faraway exotic land as a concubine. They weren't too suspicious of Mitsuha's unusual appearance.

The one thing the nobles were likely confident about was that the father doted hopelessly on the girl. What the bank manager told them about her and the display she put on with the string of necklaces all but cemented the guess. She brought the necklaces specifically to bait them…although they turned out to be much more valuable than she expected.

The nobles aren't gonna let me get away with telling them nothing, though. I have to explain myself at least a little bit. I don't want to give away anything specific. But I can't outright lie either in case our countries end up forming an amicable relationship in the future.

Mitsuha was careful with her response.

"Um, I'm not an official representative of my country… It'll be easier for me to do and say what I want here if I remain an ordinary girl from an unknown land. We can discuss my country when a member of my family or an official representative joins me. Until then, I want to learn as much as I can about this country so I can share my knowledge with everyone back home in the future."

"Hmm, I see… In that case, it'd be rude of us to pry…" one of the nobles said.

I'm glad this count can take a hint, Mitsuha thought, although she couldn't remember his name. She didn't know if he was actually convinced; he probably just figured that incurring her displeasure here would help no one.

Mitsuha was "an unofficial envoy from a country that didn't have ties to Vanel, and was here looking to start one in the future." Based on what Mitsuha just said and what the party host reiterated about her wanting to open a shop to exchange cultural ideas, the nobles should've figured that much. *Right where I want them.*

The nobles concluded it'd be easy to learn her origin with a little delving. There were a number of things they could do, such as wait for Mitsuha to slip up and speak her mother tongue, have someone tail the messenger sent from her country, or investigate the goods sold in her shop. Then, once they figured out her home country, they would feign ignorance and feed Mitsuha information about Vanel that served them.

I have nothing to worry about. No amount of investigating will tell them where I'm from. They must think I'm from a small country that has minimal diplomatic relations with Vanel and kept to itself. They're also under the impression that it's a wealthy country—or a country with wealthy royals and nobles, at least—that mass produces gemstones.

Mitsuha spent the next while making pleasant conversation with the adults—who at this point were very careful not to ask questions that could hint that they were probing about her home country or her identity. They wanted to know what kinds of things Mitsuha was interested in, which made it easy for her to steer the conversation in the direction she wanted. She was able to inquire about Vanel's naval strength, the research fleets built to expand the kingdom's territory, naval trade, and more. She also kept tabs on the names of influential nobles and high-ranking military officers who were brought up in the conversation.

You think I won't be able to remember them all? Don't worry, I prepared for that! I've got an IC recorder in my dress pocket.

Once Mitsuha felt like she had learned enough, she returned to the count's youngest daughter and brought her over to the group of children. *This is her birthday party. I'd feel terrible if she ended up getting no attention because of me, so I feel like I owe her a little. And don't tell her this, but I'm using her as a barrier to protect me from the kid missiles! The kids can't ask me questions if the star of the party is right here!*

Mitsuha decided to take her leave when it got late enough. Everyone thought she was a child, so there was nothing wrong with leaving a little early.

I would've been fine staying longer because it's not like I'm get-

ting tired. But I heard that waiting in line for the carriage to come around can take forever if you stay until the end, so I'm not gonna hesitate to use my child privilege. I constantly have to put up with the disadvantages of looking like a child, so why wouldn't I make full use of its merits too?

Knowing that no noble girl would walk home alone after a party at night—or during the day—Mitsuha had a servant summon her carriage. She would've been fine taking a horse-drawn cab, but she had her carriage driver parked in the waiting area this whole time. The hours-long charter fee was going to hurt.

Once she got back to her shop, she grabbed a wooden case full of brandy from her storage and went over to the next door. She'd bought empty seven-ounce bottles in Vanel and filled them with the alcohol purchased from Micchan's (the Japanese one) family. The case was a dozen small bottles containing three larger bottles' worth of brandy.

"Good evening! I brought this to thank you for all your hard work!" Mitsuha announced as she walked in.

Why do they look so surprised? Oh wait, I didn't change out of my dress! Yeah, I can see why they'd be taken aback...

"Sorry for coming over in my work clothes. This is brandy from my country. I brought them for you to drink after you get home... No drinking them during work, okay?"

"Th-Thank you again. You're always so kind. Are you sure you want to give these to us, though? They look really expensive..."

The six men bowed their heads gratefully.

Mitsuha was at her next-door neighbor's: the guard station. This wasn't the headquarters or a branch office. It was a small local station slightly bigger than the ones in Japan—and it was manned by six guards at night. They did their patrol rounds in shifts, but she happened to arrive when all six men were present.

I've always gotten along well with the officers at my neighborhood station. I've greeted them every day since kindergarten, and I built a good relationship with them. Even when new officers transferred in. When my uncle and his wife tried to take my house and money after my family died, and when some delinquents tried to do the same, it was the officers who helped me out. I'm forever indebted to them.

The guard station next door is partly why I chose this location. But since we're neighbors, I want to give them a little treat. Plus, I feel a little bad about essentially using them as free security.

This wasn't the first time Mitsuha had brought them gifts, but she wasn't going to do it every day, and the gifts wouldn't always be this expensive. She'd occasionally bring them late night snacks like air-fried sweet potatoes or steamed buns. If this were Japan, she might be accused of bribing the officers, but no one would say that here.

The guards probably already thought she was the daughter of wealthy merchants because she opened a shop in a prime location, but after seeing her in the dress, they now surely thought she was a noble.

And they'd be right. I jokingly called my dress "work clothes" because attending parties is work for nobles, and they didn't even react. Well, it might be for the best that they know I'm a noble. They'll probably do their best to protect me to prevent any diplomatic issues.

After that, Mitsuha jumped to her house in Japan. She needed to take her dress to the dry cleaners first thing in the morning. The nobles in the other world never wore the same dress twice. But she couldn't afford such luxuries, so she had to take care of what she had. *I'm gonna get plenty more work out of you, dress!*

...Hold on. My first dress was stained with blood, so this is all I

have left! There are also the ones I got as tribute at the World-to-World Meetings, but those aren't really... Well... They don't look like the dresses from the other world—unlike the ones made by the dressmaker—so they'd look out of place. They reveal a LOT of skin. The representatives must've assumed I'm a kid who's trying to "look grown-up." Those dresses really emphasize my chest... Were they trying to sexually harass me?!

Oh well, I guess I need to order some dresses from the degenerate dressmaker! I'm gonna be wearing dresses a lot more often from now on, so one isn't gonna cut it...

Despite what I call her, she's been really helpful. Should I upgrade her nickname? How about "Madame Degenerate"?

Chapter 45:
Gallery Café 2

Mitsuha was devoting the day to setting up her café on Earth. It wouldn't be long before nobles and their subordinates started coming to investigate her shop in the New World, but they wouldn't do so the day after the party. She hadn't even opened the business yet. The guards would surely stop anyone who tried to break in anyway, and there was nothing in the store she was worried about getting stolen. A robbery would cause her financial damage, of course, but she hadn't left any out-of-place artifacts or a hint about her true identity.

She took her dress to the dry cleaners first thing in the morning, then went to Madame Degenerate's shop and ordered a few dresses. This time, her budget was significantly higher, but it was a necessary expense. *Madame Degenerate sounds like a dominatrix but oh well.*

Once that was done, Mitsuha jumped abroad to the foundation that would keep her afloat on Earth: the gallery café (coming soon). She'd summoned her new employees to the shop.

"You two will be the team that runs my gallery café, Gold Coin," Mitsuha said. Two girls nodded in response. The three of them were inside the newly remodeled café—fully equipped and ready for busi-

ness. "These are the job details, just as I wrote on the job listing. I may be the café owner but I'm not the one who will be handling the tasks. Please tell me if you think there's anything we should change. I'll approve anything as long as all three of us agree."

She showed them a piece of paper with the working conditions written in this country's language.

"Do you have any suggestions or requests?"

Rudina   13 years old
          Manager/Chef/Accountant
          Live-in employee
          $620 per week + 10% of the café's net profit

Sylua   17 years old
          Waitress/Miscellaneous
          Commuter
          $420 per week + 10% of the café's net profit

Five-day work week. Social insurance and labor insurance supplied.
Work hours are from 10:00 AM to 6:00 PM. Breaks are allowed when appropriate. Lunch is covered.
If either employee gets sick or has to miss work for any reason, the café temporarily closes. The café shall not be run by one person alone.

Mitsuha wasn't trying to live on the profit of this café. It was the gallery that she was invested in; she was going to use it to provide herself a legal salary in Japan. She only attached the café because she couldn't leave employees to run a gallery no one would visit. She'd be grateful if they broke even on the energy bill, labor costs, material and consumable costs, and other expenses. She didn't even mind if they lost a little money. Which was why she was willing to be flexible with store hours and other details.

Thank goodness I'm exempt from taxes here... That said, if I ever lose my world-jumping ability and living situation in Japan, I can settle down here. It wouldn't be hard to reinvent the café so it makes a profit. I'll take over as the manager. I can start by folding the gallery section and converting it into customer seating.

The two girls spent a few minutes reviewing the piece of paper.

"Which two days of the week do we get off?" Rudina asked.

"Whichever days you want," Mitsuha answered. She trusted the girl's judgment.

"Hmm, I think I want Saturday and Sunday as fixed days off. We don't have a lot of seats, so we won't make much money from customers coming here to relax on the weekends. I want to target rush-hour commuters and workers on their lunch breaks who are looking for a light meal. These hours won't work for that. We'll need to do 7:00 AM to 2:00 PM, then take a break and reopen from 5:00 PM to 8:00 PM," suggested Rudina.

Holy cow, what happened to the timid little girl I interviewed? She sounds like a full-fledged businesswoman!

"You realize that would be a ten-hour workday, right?" Mitsuha asked.

"Um, yes? Is there a problem with that?"

"I guess not..."

Ten-hour workdays seemed to be the norm in this country.

"Does that sound good to you, Sylua?" Rudina asked while pointing to one particular phrase on the paper: "+ 10% of the café's net profit."

Sylua nodded vigorously. It seemed like the two of them were more focused on a hearty income than a breezy workload.

Extending your work hours won't guarantee a profit, you know? Oh well, it's not like I'll burden you with ten percent of the losses, either.

"Um…" Sylua spoke up. "If we go with these hours, can breakfast and dinner be provided too?"

She's quite tactful as well…

Mitsuha handed Rudina the keys, instructed her to finish preparing the café for the next few days before its grand opening, and gave her the money she'd need to do so. She also officially anointed the young girl as the manager of the café and gave her authority to give Sylua job-related orders. Lastly, she instructed them to craft the menu themselves while considering each item's prep time and ingredient costs. Their pay started today.

"I'm moving in tomorrow," Rudina said.

Makes sense, Mitsuha thought. *She's going to be a live-in employee.*

…Wait a second. I'm not charging her for rent or energy, she'll have free access to all the food in the café, and she's getting $620 a week. Her employment terms are way too good compared to Sylua's… It's too late to take anything from her now, though. The only thing I can do is eventually raise Sylua's salary… Damn it, why can't I do a better job of thinking this stuff through?!

Mitsuha jumped to her room on the third floor of her general store. She descended to the first floor and opened the door to her shop… and was met with a surprise.

"Mitsuha! Where did you go and why didn't you take me?!" Sabine was fuming.

Why should I have to tell you that…

Sabine had apparently gotten a report multiple days in a row from the "Mitsuha Watch Squad" that their watch target was nowhere to be seen. She'd been checking the store and calling Mitsuha on the radio every day.

…That's not my problem.

But to be fair, I've always told Sabine when I'm going away for a while. I can see why she'd be worried.

In any case, "Mitsuha Watch Squad"?! They sound sketchy! Is that why Sabine's always waiting outside the shop when I come to the capital?!

"I-I just had some business in my county—" Mitsuha began.

"That's a lie!"

Urgh, what a pain…

…Hold on. If Sabine is this upset, then… Oh God, I've got a situation here!

Sabine let out a little yelp as Mitsuha yanked her into the store. She locked the door, drew the curtains, and jumped with her.

"Mitsuha! Where did you go with Sabine?! Why did you leave me behind?!" Colette whined. They were at the Yamano County residence.

Damn it, I knew she'd be mad! This is just like that video game I played—the one where you had to keep multiple girls happy at a time or their bomb icons would get bigger and bigger and eventually blow up! What a headache!

"It's only been a few days, you two! You used to be able to go much longer without seeing me!"

The girls grew quiet.

Mitsuha did expect this. The three of them stuck together during their trip to bring countries into the alliance, and they'd grown used to each other's company. All day, every day. She couldn't blame them for having a hard time adjusting after living like that for two and a half months. They were only nine and ten, after all. And Colette was living in the Yamano County residence away from her family and fellow villagers. She had to be lonely.

But Mitsuha's activity in Vanel was top secret. She hadn't even told the king about it. She'd taken a loan from the king without explaining what she was going to use it for. Telling him would've led to him giving her orders she couldn't ignore. He would've demanded information on Vanel and its technology, and was surely going to figure out that she'd been lying about the limits of her world-jumping ability. And the biggest reason she didn't tell him was because if anything happened to her, everything would go up in smoke.

There were already going to be major impediments to building the ships and cannons if the kingdom ever lost Mitsuha. If her covert operations failed, the damage would be even bigger. Especially after getting the people's hopes up. That was why Mitsuha decided to make this a solo operation; if she failed, no one would know about it.

Taking Sabine and Colette with her was never an option. Besides, they couldn't speak the Vanelian language.

They're not going to accept getting left behind until I explain myself, though. This is a problem...

"I just have some things I need to take care of. I have a personal life too, you know!" Mitsuha said.

"Can you be more specific?" Sabine asked.

"I've, uh, been dating..."

"Don't lie!" both girls yelled.

Rude!

...I'm in a pinch. Oh, what to do, what to do? Colette is being a cranky-boo... Stop.

What should I do?

I'll tell them the truth…but only a pinch of it.

"All right. I'll show you what I've been up to!" Mitsuha grabbed the two girls' hands and jumped.

"Wh-Where are we…?" Sabine looked around. Colette couldn't manage a word.

Mitsuha had jumped the three of them into a small, enclosed space slightly over three square feet. There were no windows, but slits in the ceiling provided a little light. The room was empty except for one door.

This was a small wooden booth that Mitsuha had built and attached to the back of the gallery café, Gold Coin. She made it specifically for jumping. The gallery and the café were on the first floor of the building, and the second floor was Rudina's living space. Well, Rudina only lived in one of the rooms, and the other vacant rooms were being used to store food ingredients, unused equipment, and spare tableware. But it would've been suspicious if Mitsuha suddenly came downstairs from the second floor. Rudina and Sylua would notice that she never walked in through the front door.

Mitsuha built this external space to jump to and avoid all that mess. If a passing stranger saw her go in or out of the booth, they'd just assume it led to a back entrance into the café. It was highly unlikely Rudina or Sylua would see her back here, and if they did, she could just say she was just checking their storage. The box was perfect for camouflaging her jumps.

"Follow me!" Mitsuha opened the door and pulled the girls around the building to the café entrance. She didn't lock the jumping room from the outside. Doing so would trap her inside next time she jumped in there. There was nothing in it to protect, anyway. She would lock the jumping room from the inside when she returned to it. Not that there was any point in doing that either. It just made her feel better.

"Ta-da! You've been to Mitsuha's General Store, my county residence, my Japanese house, and now I welcome you to the fourth Yamano base—the gallery café, Gold Coin!" announced Mitsuha, gesturing to the café.

"Whaaaat?!" Sabine and Colette exclaimed. Mitsuha led the two dumbstruck girls inside.

Sylua was putting away tableware onto the shelves. "Oh, Owner. Do you need something?" Rudina was out making some final runs with the food supply dealer.

"Oh, don't mind us. I'm just showing the café to my friends," Mitsuha answered and showed the girls around the first floor, and then the second floor. She left Rudina's room out; Mitsuha owned the café, but she couldn't enter someone else's room without permission.

"Hmm…"

Sabine and Colette seemed unsure how to react. The tour of the tiny café ended quickly. They realized they weren't in Zegleus when Mitsuha and Sylua spoke an unfamiliar language. And while there was some modern cookware in the café section of the building, there wasn't anything fun like a television or DVDs—stuff that they'd find in Mitsuha's house. As a result, they didn't seem to find the place appealing.

"All right. Let's move on to the next one," Mitsuha said.

"Huh?"

Mitsuha led them out of the café, around the building, and into the jumping booth. She then locked the door and jumped.

"This is the fifth Yamano base, Yamano Commodities!"

"What…"

They were at her base in Vanel's capital, Yamano Commodities. She jumped them to the empty second floor where she was supposed to be living.

"It's empty…" Sabine said disappointedly.

Well, yeah, but that's 'cause this room is only for jumping, Mitsuha thought. *Just like the little space attached to Gold Coin.*

She brought the girls down to the as-of-yet-unopened shop on the first floor, but there was nothing to see except for a few sample goods from Zegleus and a handful of high-quality products from Japan that wouldn't be out of place in this world. There was no jewelry on display; leaving that out while the shop was unattended would be asking for it to get stolen.

"This is boring…" said Colette.

She and Sabine didn't seem impressed by the two new Yamano bases. This shop barely had anything from Earth, and Gold Coin was just a simple café. The girls also couldn't speak the language at either location. That meant they couldn't go anywhere or do anything without Mitsuha to translate. They'd both much rather spend time having fun at Mitsuha's General Store or her Japanese house.

"You two don't spend all your time playing with me, right? You're a princess, Sabine, which means you have your etiquette lessons and royal tutoring, and Colette, I know you're learning a lot from Miriam, Rachel, and Anton. There are plenty of things you guys do without me, and similarly, there are things I need to do on my own. That includes boring work stuff."

Sabine and Colette didn't say a word.

Sweet, it looks like they understand. They should be fine on their own for a little while!

Anyway, I don't need to be here right now. It's not like there are noble parties to attend in the New World every day, and I'm not ever going to spend the night here. I only have to come to Yamano Commodities every now and then. I'm not really out to make money with the shop either, so I can just open it when I have a need for it.

The top priority right now is Gold Coin's grand opening!

The opening day for the gallery café, Gold Coin, had finally arrived. Mitsuha wasn't making an event out of it. There wouldn't be much to gain from doing large-scale advertising and attracting a bunch of customers on day one. She was fine with starting modestly and gaining local popularity over time.

The café operation was entrusted to Rudina and Sylua. Mitsuha wasn't going to interfere too much. Rudina was the manager, and it was her job as the owner to observe quietly from the shadows.

The opening wasn't advertised, so Gold Coin kicked off without any crowd of customers waiting to flood inside. Mitsuha told her employees not to worry if they didn't get any customers the first few days, and that as long as the store made enough to cover business expenses and their salaries, they shouldn't have to worry about profit.

Mitsuha didn't want the café to bleed money, but she didn't mind if she lost a little. It wasn't like she was investing her future trading funds or leveraging forex gains. A small café wouldn't lose much money.

She could make up for whatever amount of money they lost with a day of business in the New World. All income made in Vanel would go into her personal savings rather than the Yamano County budget. Mitsuha didn't feel great about contributing to an enemy country's wealth by selling a lot of gold and gems, so she was going to try to hold back on those. Then again, there was only so much impact one person could have on a country's economy.

Also, Mitsuha would be satisfied as long as Gold Coin fulfilled its original purpose of sending foreign currency to Japan through legal measures so she could deposit it into her bank account. She was willing to lose a little money. The money she sent to Japan would be halved from Japanese taxes and other fees, but it would still be sufficient to cover her living expenses for the ten-plus years—until she had to leave the country because she could no longer hide her lack of aging. It would also fund her purchases of Japanese goods to sell in the other world.

Actually, I'll never have to worry about showing where I got the money for items I take to the other world. I'm not going to use any of that stuff in Japan, so people aren't going to suspect how I'm able to afford them with my declared salary.

This is not *tax evasion! I'm just abbreviating because I can't explain to anyone how I use those items!*

Mitsuha peeked into the café window from outside. There didn't seem to be any issues... Not that there'd be any issues when they hadn't gotten a single customer yet.

"Good luck, Goldy." She turned on her heel and with a swish of her skirt, she was gone.

Chapter 46:
Gathering Information

"Hello, these are for you!" Mitsuha held out eighteen rice balls she made at her house in Japan. That was more than enough for a late-night snack to feed six people.

I made them as bribe—ahem, I mean, a gift to show my appreciation for the free security service the guards are giving me. This isn't my first time bringing onigiri. They love it because it's delicious, fast to eat, and filling... Though I doubt many would complain about any snack brought over by a girl next door!

The guards delightedly accepted the onigiri and started stuffing their cheeks right away.

An older guard spoke to her. "Lady Mitsuha, we spotted a suspicious man loitering outside your shop late last night. We kept an eye on him, and he tried to break in through the back door. What a bold man to attempt a break-in right next to a guard station..."

"Holy cow! What happened?!" Mitsuha hadn't expected that. *Good thing I chose this location!*

"We captured and tortu—I mean, questioned him, and he conf—explained that he works for a viscount. The man was obviously going to sneak into your shop and commit a crime, so we contacted the viscount to come collect him, but..." the guard trailed off.

"But...?"

"The viscount sent a message saying he didn't know the man."

That's about the response I'd expect, Mitsuha thought. *It would definitely mean trouble for the viscount if it got out that a subordinate of his tried to sneak into the residence of a young woman who lives alone, or that he gave such an order.*

"We sent a message to the viscount again: 'A man of unknown origin attempting to infiltrate a foreign noble's home is a serious enough incident that requires the royal palace's immediate attention, and we must hand the criminal over to them for strict questioning. We apologize for wasting your time with something you weren't involved in.'"

"What happened after that?"

"The viscount quickly came to collect the man, and we handed him over. I thought that'd be better for your sake, rather than turning in the criminal to the royal palace and harming the reputation of the viscount's family, which might earn you his resentment." The guard grinned.

Man, these guys are good!

She didn't know if the viscount was after gemstones, information, or her own person, but messing with her in any way would've landed him in a lot of trouble in this country right now. The girl who possessed such unimaginable wealth that she was able to give pearl necklaces and artificial gems to children without a second thought. The daughter of high-ranking foreign nobles, possibly with royal blood. The parents doted on her endlessly. If the intruder revealed who he worked for during questioning, the viscount would be finished.

Knowing that, he attempted to break into my shop. What was the viscount thinking? Does he resent me, a fellow viscount, because I'm getting a lot more attention than him? Or did he want to get some information on me and make a deal? Was he after pearls or gems? I want to believe he didn't order this man to assault me.

My friendly relationship with the guards next door paid off right away! If we hadn't really spoken, they probably would've just arrested the man and dealt with him as a normal robber without bothering to go the extra mile.

The guard explained to Mitsuha that they had the viscount confirm the identity of the criminal and sign a document proving that he took him into his custody, and then submitted that to the security records in the royal palace. This guard station was in the middle of the noble district and was a part of the capital's defense force, who worked directly for the royal palace. The guards here had the authority to intervene in disputes between nobles, and they didn't cave to threats or pressure from anyone.

A noble may have been able to intimidate a guard in the commoner sections of the city into doing what they wanted, but trying that with a guard in the noble district would bring them face to face with someone high up the chain of command who could eat a low-ranking noble for lunch. That was why these guards could be so firm with nobles. They'd explained as much to Mitsuha when she brought them snacks the last time, and assured her she could rely on them.

"So if that viscount ever tries to mess with you again, tell him what we told you and that'll shut him right up. We submitted our report to the royal palace, and we have our records too. There are also plenty of eyewitnesses. No one will doubt the word of six guards protecting the noble district."

Hmm... So hypothetically, if I go to a party and blab about what the viscount did, I could ruin his life? Why would he do something so idiotic in the first place?

Oh, it's because he's an idiot... Sure, the viscount who received the peerage may have been a respected man, but there's no guarantee that his descendants wouldn't be dimwits. The viscount probably thought he could get away with doing something to a lone child who's far from home. I guess there could be one or two extreme idiots out of every few hundred nobles. The fact that there's only one is actually surprising.

But man, did the guards really think that far ahead? And take the time to fill out the paperwork and report to their bosses? I'm so grateful!

"I'll be right back!" Mitsuha exclaimed as she ran back to her shop for a quick jump to Japan.

"Sorry for the wait!"

Mitsuha returned with a box containing six bottles of brandy. Each bottle cost 4,000 yen. They were the really good ones. *I mean, uh, that's what I've heard!* This brandy was even more expensive than the vintage she poured into the six-ounce bottles. And this time, she kept them in their original twenty-four-ounce bottles.

"This is a thank-you gift for the trouble I put you through..."

"For us? A-Are you sure?" a guard sputtered. They must've really enjoyed the last batch of brandy.

"Absolutely. This brandy is much more expensive than what I brought last time. I'd say it's about two ranks higher on the luxury scale. It's really delicious... I think. I've never had it before, so I can't tell you for sure."

"Seriously?!" the guards cried in unison.

I don't like doing the whole Japanese routine of being humble and downplaying gifts. I prefer the Western way of telling the giftee how amazing it is and how excited I am to share it. It's much more fun that way! No one wants a boring gift, and I'd be offended if someone thought a cheap item would be sufficient for me.

Oh, right. There's one more thing I need to tell them.

"Don't tell anyone about this brandy. I only brought a few bottles for top-secret market research purposes before I officially put it on my shelf. If word about it leaks and some big shot demands I sell some to them in advance, I won't be able to bring you anymore. I'm gonna collect your bottles once you're done, too. Do *not* throw them away or show them to anyone. Understood?"

"Yes, Your Highness!"

Whoa, I heard that in English instead of Japanese. Weird. I wonder if the translator in my brain did that because they called me a princess half-jokingly, and it decided the best way to convey that nuance was in English? I shouldn't think too hard about it...

Six 4,000-yen bottles cost 24,000 yen altogether. That was about the worth of one gold coin when you converted it to dollars and then to yen when the exchange rate was on the lower end. Still, the cost was more than worth it as a reward to the guards who kicked the idiot viscount to the curb.

I'll have to upgrade the quality of their snacks. I should give them something else to thank them for this favor too. I sure picked the right place to rent my store space!

"By the way, Lady Mitsuha, a lot of messengers sent by nobles came to visit you. Some of them asked us where you were and when you would return, and we told them we didn't have a clue. Which was the truth, I suppose, but we wouldn't have told them even if we did know. It kinda feels like we've become your gatekeepers..." the older guard said.

Sorry, but that's exactly why I chose this place!

"Master, there's a suspicious visitor at the door..."

"A suspicious person who arrives without an appointment? Send them away! Why did you feel the need to inform me about such an elementary matter?" Marquis Mitchell scolded his gatekeeper. He wasn't thrilled about having his precious dinnertime with his family being interrupted.

This gatekeeper was no rookie, however. He was perfectly capable of judging who he should or shouldn't turn away, and he always demonstrated that. There had to be a reason he came to the marquis instead of handling it himself.

"…Describe the person to me," Marquis Mitchell said. Whoever they were, they'd have to lack all common sense to visit a noble's estate at this hour without advance notice.

"Yes, sir. It's a girl who looks around twelve or thirteen years old. She appears to be a foreigner, and her clothes are modest yet clearly upscale. And she has a message for Lady Micheline…"

That was enough for Marquis Mitchell—and his daughter Micheline, who was sitting across from him—to know who it was. "Lacking all common sense" was an appropriate way to describe her. Micheline rubbed her temples with both hands.

"…And what's the message?" the marquis asked.

"She told me to convey the following: 'Heya Micchan, let's hang out!' That is all."

Marquis Mitchell, his wife, their three sons, and their daughter Micheline all hung their heads, exasperated.

"Sorry for visiting you at this late hour," Mitsuha apologized as soon as she entered the room.

"You should be sorry…" Micchan sighed.

Geez, someone's not happy to see me! Well, it's probably because I barged my way into their home without an appointment. I can't blame them for being mad.

150

"But I didn't have any way to contact you! I came here to make an appointment in person because I didn't know any other way, but then I figured since I'm here, I might as well try to see you…"

"What noble lord would schedule an appointment herself instead of sending a servant to do it?!" Micchan huffed.

Marquis Mitchell swooped in to defend the unannounced guest. "There, there, Micheline. Don't be so hard on Viscountess Yamano. She's far from home and unaware of our customs."

Mitsuha did realize visiting this way might upset them. But she couldn't send a letter because she didn't know Micchan's address, and there were no stamps, post offices, or mailboxes here. There were no public phones or phone numbers either, obviously. The proper way to contact someone before a visit was to send a servant as a messenger and have them bring back the reply. That was how nobles did it. Like the girls in a certain yuri manga would say, "Here at the academy, we do not let our pleated skirts wrinkle or leave our shirt collars lopsided."

"I brought gifts!" Mitsuha declared as she set her shoulder bag and handheld bag on the table and opened them. She brought Marquis Mitchell the same 4,000-yen brandy she gave the guards, and for Micchan, some Japanese confectionery. Mitsuha carefully selected fifteen cakes from the Japanese pastry chain Châteraisé to make up what she called the Mitsuha Collection.

"Is this…" Marquis Mitchell trailed off.

"Yes, it is brandy from my country," answered Mitsuha. "I'd like to hear what you think of it. And Micchan, I made you some cakes from my country. If you could also give your thoughts and tell me if you think they would sell in this country, I would appreciate it…"

I couldn't tell them I brought fresh-baked cakes all the way from my homeland, so I had to say I made them myself. There's no other way to

explain how they could be here right now. I could've given them some-thing that keeps well like cookies, but cookies are common here and they just wouldn't have had the same impact. Lying was my only choice!

Oh, but Micchan will get fat if she eats all these cakes herself... I didn't think about that. Or maybe she'll get diarrhea and actually lose weight.

The family stared at the brandy and cakes in silence until Mar-chioness Mitchell ordered a maid to fetch some tableware.

Is Micchan going to eat the cakes right away? The gatekeeper told me they just had dinner—oh, right, dessert stomach. Might as well call it a double stomach.

Huh? The marquis is having some cake too? With brandy? Interest-ing... Wait, I've actually heard that brandy goes well with slightly sweet foods. I read an article once about how some people enjoy their Valen-tine's Day chocolate and cakes with brandy.

The entire family was voraciously eyeing Micchan's cakes. The girl and her mother looked especially ravenous. Mitsuha had in-tended the cakes for Micchan, but given how appetizing the cakes looked, she could hardly blame the rest of the family for wanting a piece too. There wasn't a person alive who could look at these cakes and not want to devour them.

Châteraisé is a powerhouse!

Micchan quickly realized she wouldn't be able to eat all fifteen cakes herself and looked a bit mopey. Her family wasn't going to allow that, and she couldn't have gotten to all of them before they went bad, anyway.

After a family debate among the Mitchells, it was decided that Micchan would have four cakes, Marchioness Mitchell would have three cakes, and Marquis Mitchell and the three sons would each have two cakes. They fought quite a lot to reach that compromise, and the arguing didn't stop there. The guys wanted everyone to take turns picking one cake each until they reached their allotted amount, but the ladies (Micchan and Marchioness Mitchell) were adamant that they get to pick all of their cakes before the guys got a turn. If they did as the guys said, the girls would be forced to choose between the three least popular cakes at the end.

"These cakes were a present for me! Why should I have to choose between the last three that no one wants! You all should be happy you're getting any at all! Father, I don't see you sharing your gift with the rest of us!"

Holy cow, I thought Micchan was the calm and collected type, Mitsuha thought. *Were the cakes so enticing that they corrupted her? Maybe it was a bit of an overkill…*

"W-Well, that's because you all aren't ready for such strong alcohol…" Marquis Mitchell argued, to which his wife responded by slamming down an empty glass in front of him.

I suppose I should've seen this coming. They're not sharing any with me. I don't mind that because the cakes and brandy were a gift for the family. The empty spot on the table in front of me is a little depressing, though…

Just as Mitsuha was thinking that, a maid brought her a plate of scone-like desserts and a cup of black tea.

Man, skilled maids are just different!

"…So, would you be willing to help me decide which parties I should and shouldn't attend, and educate me on this country's etiquette?" Mitsuha asked Marquis Mitchell after the guys finished their cakes. This was the main purpose behind her visit.

Marquis Mitchell, who had been swirling his brandy-filled glass under his nose and enjoying the aroma, answered without even looking at Mitsuha. "Hmm. If you want to learn our etiquette, you could start by refraining from nighttime visits without an appointment."

My bad!

"With one exception…"

"Yeah?"

"If you bring this brandy and these cakes on your visit."

All right, all right. I wonder if he means he's willing to forgive my rudeness this time, or if he's telling me to bring brandy and cakes next time too?

Or both? Okay then. Did my gifts really have that big of an impact? If a marquis enjoyed the brandy this much, I wonder how the guards felt about it… I'm scared of their reaction the next time I see them!

Unlike the guys, Micchan and Marchioness Mitchell were still savoring their cakes. They looked like they were in seventh heaven.

Is Micchan mellowing out? Will she warm up to me now?

No? Fine.

"Moving on. Viscountess Yamano, are you asking what I think you're asking?" Marquis Mitchell's expression switched from lax to serious.

It was important that they were on the same page. Mitsuha was asking a marquis who likely belonged to a major faction—actually, he probably *ran* the faction—to help her decide who she should get acquainted with. No noble would fail to recognize the meaning behind that question. Aside from the types who were dumb enough to send a pawn to snoop around her shop.

"…Yes." The viscountess nodded firmly.

"Mitsuha…" Micchan stopped eating her cake and leered at her friend. "Did you use me as an excuse to come over? You really just wanted to scheme with Father!"

Ah, what a perceptive girl… I like you!

Mitsuha nonchalantly ignored the peeved girl and continued her conversation with the marquis. Negotiating with other nobles was part of Mitsuha's job as the head of a noble family, and as a smart girl with a noble education, Micchan was well aware of that. Which was why she wasn't too mad. She knew not to get involved in their business affair.

"That, and... I have an interest in this country's ships," Mitsuha continued. "I want to know things like how much cargo they can carry, and at what speed and cost. What the odds are of losing vessels, cargo, and crew to pirates or maritime accidents. And, um..."

"Go on," the marquis urged.

"In the event of a crisis in my country, would we be able to count on Vanel's navy to help us?"

Mitsuha gave a lot of thought as to how to ask about Vanel's military and ships without drawing suspicion, and that was what she came up with. Marquis Mitchell paused and pondered for a bit.

"Hmm, those are difficult questions..." he began. "Some merchants have their own ships while others rely on shipping companies. The vessels themselves vary, as well as the ships' crews. That's not to mention the things that could affect the likelihood of an accident or a pirate attack: the route, the type of boat, the size of the fleet, the weather, and the season. It's too complicated to give you any hard numbers."

Oh, that makes sense.

"And I couldn't possibly speak on the likelihood of Vanel offering your country support. That would depend on a number of factors including what kind of treaty the two countries have, how broadly we want to interpret it, our current diplomatic relationship, and the national and international climates."

I see, I see!

Mitsuha decided not to ask any more direct questions about the functionality of the ships for now. She could learn enough from investigating the captured ships and asking the former prisoners who were now citizens of Zegleus. Barring a major technological breakthrough, it was highly unlikely the new ships were dramatically superior to the old ones. At the end of the day, sailing ships were sailing ships.

She had also already learned a decent amount about the state-of-the-art ships from the soldier boy, and it wouldn't be too hard to find him again. He was only a lowly sailor—or maybe a junior candidate for an officer position—but she thought she could trust his knowledge about ships. After all, it was the sailors who measured the ship's speed with chip logs, operated the sails, and actually ran the ships.

As such, it'd be pointless to query the marquis about the ships. He wasn't an expert. She decided to refrain from asking about Vanel's foreign policy too; questions like "How likely would Vanel be to invade if they discovered a new continent?" would give away too much. She'd need to find the right person at the right moment to ask that.

Mitsuha decided to spend the rest of the evening with small talk.

"How long would it take for your country to send cargo to Vanel using its ships?" Marquis Mitchell asked.

Whoa, I see what you're doing there! Answering that question would tell him how far away my country is. That would narrow down the list of likely countries. Admitting that we have ships would let him know it borders the ocean, too.

Mitsuha knew exactly how to answer. "Hmm, it's too complicated to give you any hard numbers." She threw the marquis's words right back at him.

"…Ah. I see."

"Indeed."

Marquis Mitchell and Mitsuha both burst out laughing.

"Hey, stop leaving me out of your own little world!"

Oh no, Micchan's pouting! I need to cheer her up! She's my first and only friend in this land.

What about the birthday girl I gave the necklace to, you ask? I only gave her that as a gift to thank the count's family for inviting me to my first party in Vanelian high society, and to make the bank president who introduced me look good. My main goal was to give everyone the impression that I'm a naive, sheltered girl who'd be beneficial to accommodate. The birthday girl was nothing more than a pawn for my performance. She has nothing on Colette and Sabine, who've braved through life-threatening situations with me, or Micchan, who saved me from a pinch with a dirty joke.

There's a chance we could become real friends in the future, but that hasn't happened yet. Also, I'm a little ticked off that her dad tried to force me and Micchan into making friends. If I let him strong-arm me into a friendship with his daughter, other nobles will think I'm a pushover and come at me with similarly forceful methods. I need to show that I won't associate with anyone who ignores my wishes or spreads misinformation. I feel bad for the girl, though…

Long story short, Micchan is my only real friend in this country right now. She went out of her way to tell a boob joke—which she couldn't have liked doing—to save me when I was about to lose my mind from embarrassment. Without knowing that I would give her my ruby necklace to thank her.

She was the only person in the room who looked at me without a hint of greed and bore herself as a proper noble.

For the rest of the evening, Mitsuha chatted with Micchan, her parents, and her three brothers, doing her best to steer the conversation toward the topics she was interested in. They did the same, though, subtly laying traps for Mitsuha to get caught in. Her social status, her position, her family, anything that would narrow down her home country. They even tried to bait her into accidentally uttering words in her native tongue.

Talk about exhausting!

Not wanting to stay too late, Mitsuha made her way out of the Mitchell estate. *Well, it was already way too late when I arrived... Whoops...* In any case, she was able to ask the type of questions she couldn't ask strangers at a party and gained a lot of new information.

Marquis Mitchell wouldn't have shared so much with her if he didn't think of her as an ally. Or at least, an ally while in this country. There was no reason for them to be enemies given that Mitsuha didn't know any other Vanelian nobles yet. Besides, she was friends with Micchan.

...We are friends, right?

Marquis Mitchell was well aware that his peerage and influence in political and business circles made him an appealing character. Which was why he wasn't surprised when Mitsuha chose him to butter up to.

People with self-confidence are something else! If someone tried to cozy up to me, I'd spend the whole time wondering about their ulterior motives. Tales of my paranoia would get passed down in legend!

That said, the marquis probably only thought of Mitsuha as an ally regarding domestic matters; she'd side with her country in international affairs. Vanel was a powerful country. No small nation that hadn't even established trade would act hostile toward it for no reason. It made more sense for her country to secure diplomatic relations and trade, and curry favor in the hopes of becoming an ally someday. They might even send a beautiful, illegitimate princess to pave that road.

…That's probably what he thinks I am. Hey, don't comment on the "beautiful" part!

Marquis Mitchell was probably acting friendly and lenient toward her because he didn't want to scare her away by asking too many questions and risk her joining an enemy faction. That was just Mitsuha's conjecture, though.

Mitsuha learned during their conversation that Marquis Mitchell's influence in the military was in the army rather than the navy.

Darn! It would've been convenient if it was the navy… Or maybe not? Being connected to an army faction might have its benefits. Members of the navy might be more willing to laugh it off if a little girl in the army faction says something ignorant. And they might be more willing to entertain a child's innocent curiosity.

This might actually work out.

"All right, I'll send for your carriage," Marquis Mitchell said.

"Oh, I walked here, so I don't have a carriage. I'm gonna walk back, too."

"WE'RE NOT GOING TO LET A GIRL WALK HOME ALONE AT NIGHT!" all of the Mitchells shouted.

Man, Micchan's family is in sync…

Chapter 47:
Rudina

Rudina was twelve years old when she had to leave the orphanage. She didn't blame the facility; it could only support so many children at a time. Her departure would make room for another small child to be taken in.

Rudina herself was probably only allotted a spot in the orphanage at age four because someone else gave up theirs. That being so, she felt nothing but gratitude toward the orphanage. Twelve was an old enough age to support oneself—at least compared to when she was four, dumpster diving in back alleys. That was for sure.

The orphanage didn't just boot out children and let them fend for themselves, of course. Whenever a child had to leave, the director used his connections to find them a job. He got her work as a live-in assistant at a shop. Unfortunately, her employer paid her a slave's wage and gave her slop to eat and a thin blanket to stay warm with.

The job wasn't all bad, though. It beat picking through garbage, at least. She just had to bear it until she turned fifteen, when she'd be free from the need to live under a guardian. More jobs would open up for her, and she could leave this terrible shop that took advantage of orphans.

Her boss surely thought he could exploit her forever. But she wasn't an idiot. She spent her time outside of work studying to gain business skills. She was grateful to the orphanage director for teaching her to read and write. She swore to return the favor one day.

Three years of patience. That was all that stood between Rudina and freedom. She would use that time to study and prepare herself for adult life.

Her plans went up in smoke when the shop went bankrupt a year later.

A-hah… Ahahaha! Ahahahahahaha!

All she could do was laugh in her despair.

There were no decent places to get a job at thirteen. The best you could hope for was an unpaid apprenticeship that offered food, but the majority of those jobs were taken by children who got in through connections. An orphan with nobody to rely on had little chance of securing one. The only ways such children could support themselves were by pickpocketing, thievery, or prostitution.

Two more years. Rudina somehow needed to last just two more years until she could get a normal job. She wanted to avoid sullying herself with thievery or prostitution, but if that was an option for her, she never would've planned to put up with three years at the shop. She would've quit within the first week.

This country placed little value on human lives. Especially the lives of orphans. The wages for their labor reflected that.

It'd been three days since Rudina's boss fled the shop in the middle of the night, forcing her to venture out on her own with only enough money to buy less than a week's worth of bread. She was looking for a job but had gotten rejected everywhere she went.

The orphanage had gotten her an underage work permit, but her boss confiscated it and never returned it before he fled. He didn't want her using it to find a different job. She didn't know if he forgot to give it back, if he simply didn't have time while he packed his getaway bag, if he planned to falsify it and use it to exploit a street urchin, or if he intended to sell it to a forger. Whatever the case, she wasn't getting the permit back.

She couldn't bring herself to ask the orphanage to get another one issued for her. You couldn't get any kind of permit at a government office without a bribe, and reissuing a lost permit required an even larger sum.

This country had passed a law—probably to bootlick some developed countries—that forbade children under fifteen from working without a permit or a guardian's permission. But the law didn't exactly work as intended. What usually ended up happening was the "guardian" would confiscate the permit and work the child for free, giving them nothing but the bare necessities to survive.

Allowing a child to work without a permit put both the employee and employer in danger of getting in serious trouble. The only way to avoid arrest if you were caught was to pay a massive bribe. Not many employers were willing to take that risk. Anyone willing to hire a child would more than likely subject them to illegal or unsavory work.

Prohibiting children under fifteen from working without a good reason—that law probably did protect children in developed countries. But in a country like this, it just restricted them and made them targets for exploitation.

The leaders of this country likely knew what they were doing when they passed the law. They succeeded in delighting whatever first-world organization that fought for human rights while the rich—business owners who endorsed low-wage child labor and government employees who accepted bribes—only got richer.

Those people can all go to hell!

When Rudina only had enough change left for four more pieces of bread, she came across a flier. It said, "Seeking gallery café employees at Gold Coin." It was a perfectly ordinary job posting, except for one detail. The sentence that every job posting included—the one requiring the candidate to be fifteen or older—was missing.

Rudina figured they just forgot it. But even then, she couldn't help but feel a little hopeful.

"U-Um, Rudina... How old are you?" the interviewer asked.

"I'm thirteen!" Rudina answered.

"Why did you apply to this café?"

"Because there was no age requirement on the application!"

The interviewer turned out to be a girl younger than Rudina. She probably had rich parents and was opening a café for fun. But Rudina didn't care. All that mattered was finding a job so she could make enough money to live. She was willing to sign a contract with the devil to achieve that.

The interviewer froze up at Rudina's answer. *So she did just forget...*

"...U-Um, should I not have applied?"

The interviewer snapped out of her shock. "You circled both the manager and the waitress position on your application. Do you know how to cook?"

"More or less... I'm good at math too."

"You two will be the team that runs my gallery café, Gold Coin."

Am I dreaming?

This must be a mistake, Rudina thought when she received the hiring notice. The risk of hiring a child under fifteen was too great.

Rudina was honest about her age during the interview because she knew it would only become a problem if she was hired. She told the owner that she grew up in an orphanage, that her boss didn't return her underage work permit after his store went bankrupt, and that she didn't want to trouble the orphanage by asking for another one. She was sure that only a criminal organization or a brothel would hire her after hearing all of that.

All the other applicants were over fifteen. Hiring them would've been no issue. Why did the owner choose her? Was "gallery café" a fancy way of saying brothel?

"These are the job details, just as I wrote on the job listing... Please tell me if you think there's anything we should change."

The owner left a pile of money on the table and instructed Rudina and her coworker to use it to prepare the café's opening. She didn't even make them write a receipt.

Was this girl an idiot?

...Rudina and Sylua, her new seventeen-year-old subordinate, stared at the money in disbelief. It seemed like the owner was serious. Three long minutes passed before Rudina finally spoke up.

"She really trusts us, huh..."

"Yes, I think so..." Sylua gulped.

Rudina turned to Sylua. "That owner is inarguably a good-natured person who is naive about the world. Anyone who betrays her kindness is my sworn enemy," she warned, making her feelings clear.

Sylua grinned fiercely in response. "I feel the same way."

Oh, I see. I'm not the only one who the owner saved from a hopeless dead end. Or the only one who pretended to be a harmless, timid girl, for that matter...

"Let's give this job everything we have. We'll build a loyal customer base, make a profit, and drive away any enemies who would threaten the business. We won't disappoint the owner. Does that sound good?"

"I wouldn't have it any other way!"

And so, their battle began.

The owner came back three days later.

"This is for you," she said, handing Rudina her underage work permit. They spent the next few minutes chatting and getting to know each other, and Rudina learned that the owner was also making her own way in the world after losing her family.

Rudina called Sylua over when the owner left.

"I want to amend the mission statement I gave you a few days ago."

"…How so?"

"I'm changing 'drive away any enemies who would threaten the business, and don't disappoint the owner' to 'crush our enemies and make the owner happy.'"

"…I wouldn't have it any other way!"

Chapter 48:
Business

"...And confirm purchase."

Mitsuha was at Gold Coin, buying products on Colette's Sculptures online store. She had converted one of the empty rooms on the second floor into an office. *Cafés don't stand a chance these days without online advertising.*

That was her excuse for setting up the computer in the office, but her true purpose was to buy sculptures from her Japanese company's website and leave evidence of the transactions. She needed a front to explain how she was making so much money at her age so the tax office and whatnot wouldn't get suspicious.

I bet they'll never expect me to over-report on my taxes instead of under-report! Mwahahaha! Sigh...

Today, Mitsuha bought a stone sculpture and a wooden sculpture she procured in the other world, as well as an impossibly-made sculpture (with her world-jumping ability): a complexly intertwined stone carving.

Man, the sculpture I made is unreal. There's no way it could've been made with normal techniques! They put the Mitchell-Hedges crystal skull to shame!

Mitsuha acquired the wooden sculptures from Lortor and the stone sculptures from Tiras. They were the two young artists who visited Mitsuha's General Store to plead for her patronage. She'd bought them for a few small gold coins to just less than one gold coin. Their prices at the gallery café would be equivalent to 10,000 yen per small gold coin that she paid.

The exchange rate of 10,000 yen would be four small gold coins if you converted the currency of the other world based on the gold content in the metal, but Mitsuha was converting them based on how much the money "felt" like they were worth. Going by the average salary and living expenses in either world, four small gold coins would buy 40,000-yen worth of goods. She set the prices based on "feel".

Truthfully, you couldn't apply the same feeling-based exchange rate to everything. Wheat and vegetables were much cheaper in the other world, while clothes and luxuries were more expensive. Art fell into the latter category but art pieces from unknown novices sold for way less than they did on Earth, so it evened out; 10,000 yen per small gold coin felt fair.

Mitsuha spent a little time researching the market price for art, but she was still an amateur in that field, so she decided not to think too hard about it. There was no point in comparing the market prices between the worlds, anyway. If anyone was willing to buy the pieces at the prices she set, that was good enough for her. She would reconsider the price of anything that didn't sell. It's not like she needed the money right away to support herself.

I can take it easy on this business.

Those were just the prices at Gold Coin, though. Colette's Sculptures would mark up the price by ten times and Mitsuha would purchase them herself through Gold Coin. Otherwise, she'd have to make multiple small transactions to meet the large sum she was trying to wire to Japan. Gold Coin didn't have space to display that many sculptures, anyway.

The Japanese tax office was unlikely to take issue with her selling the sculptures for exorbitant prices and paying a lot of taxes. Gold Coin would be purchasing those items and selling them at a massive loss, but Mitsuha was exempt from taxes in this country. She doubted she'd have to submit a financial statement. Her exemption from taxes was why she was able to set up this project, and the biggest reason why she chose this country to start the café.

Small, accommodating countries rock! You could say I'm thanking the people of this country by offering art and café service at a massive loss...

If this were Japan, operating a business on such an absurd loss margin would definitely lead to an investigation. No one would intentionally set prices that would lose them a significant amount of money without a reason, and that reason was almost certain to be nefarious...

A few days later, Mitsuha transported a collection of sculptures, paintings, and other knickknacks into Gold Coin.

I jumped them here, obviously. I wouldn't go through the trouble of shipping them all the way from Japan. I don't think I'll need a receipt to claim I shipped them and write the shipping fees off as an expense. If that doesn't work, whatever. I'm not going to actually ship items just to get a receipt. Writing something off as an expense doesn't get you that money back, anyway; the tax office simply deducts the charge from your return.

Shipping items overseas involves packing, writing the address, and filling out paperwork. There are too many steps. Hooray for my world-jumping ability!

Mitsuha displayed the sculptures on pedestals and spaces she had prepared and hung the paintings on the wall. She was selling more than just the strange sculptures she made with her world-jumping ability and the sculptures she bought from the artists from the other world—she did a little online-shopping on Earth and in-store shopping in the other world for anything that caught her eyes. It would be conspicuous if Colette's Sculptures was the only supplier in her records, so she wanted to show it was just one supplier of many. She didn't expect those items to be popular either. But purchasing them was a necessary expense to deflect attention from Colette's Sculptures. As long as one sold every now and then, that was good enough for her.

The café part of the business would provide enough money to maintain the shop and pay the employees' salaries, so it didn't matter to Mitsuha if she lost a little money overall. As long as she could send enough money to Japan to replenish what she spent using her Japanese bank account, it was fine. No one would bat an eye at her for spending a few years living off her parents' money, especially if she could prove she had a job.

"Perfectamundo! All right, starting tomorrow, Gold Coin will sell art too! If you make a sale, please take care of it for me!" Mitsuha told her employees.

She had explained to Rudina, the store's manager, how to sell the art pieces. Each item had a price tag, and just to be safe, there was also a notebook by the register listing all the prices. Just in case a customer tried to rewrite the price on the tag.

One concern was the large amount of cash that would go into the register after a piece was sold. A café run by two young girls would be easy picking for a robber. There were no night safes in the vicinity, and even if there were, Mitsuha didn't want Rudina walking the streets alone at night with a sack of money after closing. There were plenty of people in the world who'd kill to steal as little as seven, eight bucks.

Not everywhere in the world had low crime rates like Japan. Even developed countries like the United States had dangerous areas. Mitsuha installed a security system for that reason. She made other preparations like visiting the local police station—gift in hand—to inform them of the café's grand opening.

The most important precaution, however, was making sure that Rudina and Sylua knew not to take unnecessary risks. They could always make more money. There was no reason to get killed over ten or twenty dollars. She told them not to resist too much if a customer stole something, dined and dashed, or did anything else threatening—to think only of their own and their customers' safety, and that she would make anyone who stole from them regret it later. Mitsuha also trained them in Japanese-style customer service.

They can handle themselves from here!

"...What the heck? Someone actually bought something from Colette's Sculptures? Why?"

To Mitsuha's shock, someone ordered one of the sculptures on her website where the prices were over ten times higher than at Gold Coin. She never thought for a second that it'd actually happen.

What idiot would do that?! I have to deal with overseas shipping now, damn it. Should I make up some reason to cancel their order? Tell them we're out of stock?

By the way, the order is for one of the sculptures I made... Why, yes. Yes, I am flattered.

Business

Well, there's nothing for it. I'll give them a discount to commemorate the launch of the company, and I'll even throw in a freebie!

...Why did they just order another one?! Are they messing with me?!

Chapter 49:
The Life of a Degenerate Woman

Her name was Noriko Kishiyama. Some called her by the nickname of Kishy, and others by Hime-Kishi, meaning "princess knight," because of her prowess at cosplaying as a princess knight in armor. She began cosplaying in the early days of the trend, so her version of a princess knight was not the popular kind we see today, but instead what was colloquially known as "bikini armor."

Over time, Noriko branched out to less revealing costumes. All of her outfits were made by hand. A few friends she met at Comiket asked her to make them some Sailor Toon costumes, where she displayed her exceptional talent. This led to other cosplayers requesting outfits from her as well. That experience awakened her to the thrill of creating bespoke costumes for others and witnessing them come to life on the models. But as she got olde—err, lost the time to cosplay, she devoted herself more and more to custom-making for cosplayers who are young—err, not good at sewing.

By the time she withdrew from the front line as a cosplayer, she was ready to open her own shop. She hadn't spent all her time on cosplay; she also worked her regular job and studied her craft.

The regular job was her shop: Dresses for Maidens. It was a

normal dressmaking shop most of the time, but she accepted cosplay projects upon request. The materials she used depended on the customer's budget, but she never cut corners on production, even if the customer had a limited budget and requested inexpensive materials. A cultured maiden like herself would never do any less.

Noriko worked on lackluster projects to support herself while spending her days looking forward to the occasional creatively inspiring gig—passion projects that she wouldn't even mind doing for free. She fantasized that, one day, a dream job would fall into her lap... Something that would enable her to exercise the full scope of her talent without any worry for budgets.

But it was just that: a fantasy. For a small-town dressmaker, a pipe dream.

Until one day...

"Hellooo, can you please make me a dress?! It needs to be nice enough to wear at a foreign noble's party. You don't have to worry about the budget. I need it ASAP!"

"Wh... Wh-Wh-Wh-What did you say?!"

Mitsuha—a girl who grew up in Noriko's neighborhood—had just uttered the unbelievable.

A noble party? Just to warn you, I'm going to make this dress out of the very finest silk.

Huh? That's good with you?! Seriously?!

You're giving me this much *as an advance payment,* and *you're leaving the design entirely to me?!*

Hell yeah! I won't let you down!

Noriko finished the perfect dress after pulling many all-nighters. She hadn't been that fired up about a job in years. Passion coursed through her veins as she worked. She could put up with another three years of boring, regular dressmaking jobs after this.

Mitsuha gave her a report shortly afterward.

What?! The people from abroad loved the dress so much they gave you a lucrative sponsorship?!

Whoa! Whoawhoawhoa!

Noriko decided to close the shop early that day and splurge on half a month's worth of her food budget to celebrate with French cuisine. The name of the French restaurant is, of course, Sucre. She called Chef Kanai and made a reservation.

I'm having a full-course dinner paired with sparkly white Veuve Clicquot!

Oh, what an incredible day that was... I might never get another job like that in my life...

"Hellooo, can you please make some dresses for a foreign noble lady's debutante ball? This is a very important job. You could end up ruining her life if the dresses aren't up to par. She'll need three outfits, and the budget is unlimited... That said, I'd rather you not go crazy and spend something like three million yen..." It was Mitsuha again.

Is this actually happening?!

"Wh-Wh-What an honor! What bliss!" Noriko cried, giving the girl a tight squeeze without thinking.

Oooh, this is a nice perk—not now, Noriko!

This is the dream job I've been waiting for! I never thought it would come true! I, Noriko Kishiyama, am going to make dresses for a foreign noble lady's debutante ball! I just can't believe it!

This is a once-in-a-lifetime chance. I'm going to give every fiber of my being to this project and show them what Japanese people are capable of! Watch out, world! You shall witness the blazing soul of Noriko

Kishiyama!

Huh? You're doing a play? And the theme is knight in armor? Oh, me, me, me! That's my expertise!

Noriko got so excited she had to take a few deep breaths to calm herself.

Sword? Yes, of course I'll take care of that too! Just make sure you take pictures! And get it on video if you can! I'll give you a discount!

Oh, and it'd be nice if I could meet the lady. That would help me come up with the perfect designs for her. And since she's a foreigner, I'll need to know about her country's unique trends and styles. It's important I be familiar with the country's standards too, such as whether you can show any leg, and how much skin is appropriate.

I want to see as many pictures of sample dresses as you can take to use as reference. Can you do that for me, Mitsuha? You can? Hell yeah!

Noriko asked Mitsuha to get the pictures as quickly as possible.

"Wow, wow, WOW!" Noriko squealed.

Mitsuha brought the foreign noble lady over to Dresses for Maidens.

But why is she blindfolded? Let me see her face...

Mitsuha removed the cloth over the guest's eyes.

"NOW THAT'S WHAT I CALL A BABE!"

Noriko set about taking the girl's measurements and chatted with her through Mitsuha the interpreter.

Oh, I'm so glad to be alive... My soul! My blood! I can feel the passion coursing!

I've still got it in me!

Mitsuha gave Noriko a memory card before she left. Noriko opened the files right away on her computer. There were photos of dresses displayed in boutiques, dresses spread out on beds, and to her amazement, there were many photos of girls modeling their dresses.

OH MY GOD THEY'RE SO CUTE! They even posed and smiled for the camera... Thank you so much, Mitsuha! You're my favorite person ever! I've got your back for the rest of my life!

It'd been seven days since Noriko delivered Mitsuha the dresses. She poured her heart and soul into each one and was proud of how they turned out. The party should've already happened, and she was expecting Mitsuha to arrive at any moment.

"Hellooo—"

FINALLY!

Noriko snatched the memory card from Mitsuha's hands before she even finished her hello and sprinted to the computer. Her hands were shaking so much she had trouble inserting the card.

Come on... There we go!

Noriko worked her way through the photos.

Drip.

Oh, my nose is bleeding...

Drip.

Whoops, I'm drooling...

Drip.

Damn it, am I crying...?

OMIGOD OMIGOD OMIGOD! The dresses were a hit! Noriko thought as she watched the girl receive high praise from the foreign nobles while wearing her dresses. She didn't need to understand the language to understand their reactions.

I've never felt so fulfilled...

Mitsuha was right behind her saying something, but the dressmaker couldn't care less. She was too occupied basking in her overwhelming joy.

Noriko sent Mitsuha an email. The girl was away from home often and difficult to reach, so that seemed like the surest way to contact her.

"When's my next gig for a noble lady?!" Noriko wrote.

She also found out that Mitsuha was calling her the "degenerate dressmaker," so she complained about that.

"Do you take me for a weirdo who's into yaoi?! I like *yuri*, not yaoi! Never call me a degenerate again!"

...If you want, Mitsuha, you can call me your grande sœur.

Chapter 50:
More Parties

Mitsuha was at a party. The host was a count who belonged to a navy faction. Marquis Mitchell scored her an invitation, despite belonging to an army faction himself. She'd mentioned wanting to meet a noble from a navy faction, so he reached out to a count he was on good terms with. The count, who was a key member of the navy faction, was throwing a party for his son's promotion.

The son was being promoted to captain and had been put in command of a four-warship unit. That was certainly cause for celebration. The son was actually in his late forties; he'd be a count already if not for his long-living father.

The count was apparently thrilled that Marquis Mitchell had reached out for Mitsuha to attend his party. Members of navy factions and army factions weren't exactly close. Meanwhile, navy factions were hostile amongst themselves. The same went for the army factions. Compared to that, Marquis Mitchell and the count's relationship would be considered downright friendly. According to the Thirty-Six Stratagems, you should befriend distant states and strike your neighbors.

It always feels nice to receive kindness from an unexpected source.

The marquis is probably rubbing his hands together and tittering, "All according to plan." He's not here today, though.

There were way too many parties for each noble to attend every single one. That would mean attending dozens of parties every day, each one with thousands of attendees. Well, maybe not thousands; parties where the whole family would attend were rare.

There were hundreds of noble families that passed down their peerage, which meant there were thousands of nobles. It was harrowing to think about how many birthday parties there'd be in a year, not to mention other kinds of events. That was why nobles only attended parties when they knew the host or had a reason to go. Rank, faction, and other factors could influence that decision. At the end of the day, nobles didn't actually attend that many parties, and the number of attendees at a party could vary greatly.

Children's birthday parties were a whole different beast. Nobles attended those regardless of faction if they had an offspring close in age to the birthday child, and they brought their entire family. As a result, they could be quite large in scale.

Oh yeah, the marquis told me not to attend any more children's birthday parties for the foreseeable future. There are apparently rumors swirling that I'll give gems of unimaginable value as a reward to anyone who invites me to one. On top of that, nobles of lower rank are all chomping at the bit to hitch me to their third or fourth son. Needless to say, I'm gonna pass. I have no interest in getting married yet.

There was also a gargantuan number of birthday parties, which meant the attendees were usually limited to families who were close to the hosts or had children of the appropriate age. It would just be awkward if Mitsuha went. To make matters worse, her inability to attend all of them meant she would have to pick and choose, and her lack of a parent would make it seem like it was her own decision to attend the birthday party—out of an interest in the birthday boy.

Yep, you can count me out of kids' birthday parties!

From what Mitsuha heard, the bank president chose the last party because it was coming up, and he thought her first party would be difficult if she was the only child in a sea of adults. Making conversation was also generally easier at a child's birthday party.

He put a lot of thought into that, didn't he. I knew I could count on him! I wouldn't have met Micchan and Marquis Mitchell without his help. I'll have to give him something to thank him. Brandy would probably work. It's cheap and I'm sure he'll appreciate it.

Anyway, considering the purpose of today's party, Mitsuha guessed that most of the attendees would be high-ranking nobles from navy factions and senior naval officers. The party would be relatively small, and there would be hardly any young people...aside from Mitsuha. But she was there as the head of a noble house, not a daughter of a noble; she was an exception.

Long story short, the count who was hosting the party was overjoyed that Mitsuha chose to attend, and he was grateful to Marquis Mitchell for mediating. Technically, the marquis was the one who chose the party; Mitsuha still didn't know left from right in Vanelian high society.

Why is he so happy I chose his party, anyway... Eh, I shouldn't think too hard about it.

"There really is no better food for strong, seafaring men than half-rotten pickled pork, rock-hard bread infested with weevils, and bean soup that tastes like nothing but salt! Throw in a half-pint of rum for outstanding service and you're golden!"

"Wahaha! I like you, li'l missy!"

Yup, I'm really popular! Among smelly old men, that is. If only they were the elegant, rugged type of older men that I like. These guys are nothing like the fit, keen-eyed, resilient classic seafarers you see in movies.

Mitsuha heard a lot about the food sailors ate at sea from the former prisoners. Sailors' living conditions are more or less the same in both worlds. Fortunately, there was no vitamin B1 deficiency in this world like in the Japanese navy.

There weren't many young women who could keep up with navy nuts in conversation, let alone ask engaging questions. It was no surprise they took to Mitsuha like they did.

I wonder if that sailor boy will look like these men in a few decades. Oh, I should probably meet with him soon. I could see him becoming a lieutenant in a decade or so. That'll make him a valuable source of information.

I get the feeling that he's no ordinary sailor. He seemed smart and well-educated. No offense to other sailors...

"Hmm, that doesn't sound right to me," Mitsuha said. "I don't think your opponent lost and fled because they approached leeward. They approached leeward because they intended to flee from the beginning, probably because they thought they had no chance against a Vanelian fleet..."

"Hey, that's what we said! Our commander was baffled by their withdrawal 'cause he couldn't imagine a fleet commander makin' such a cowardly move. We told the commander the same thing, and he said, 'don't stoop to insults just because they're our enemies.' So you had the same thought as us, li'l missy. Bwahaha!"

The nobles were calling Mitsuha "Viscountess Yamano" at first, but they dropped that in favor of "li'l missy" once the alcohol went to their heads.

Will you quit smacking me on the back like that, guys?! That really hurts!

This serves me perfectly, though. If the men are this drunk and jovial...

"By the way, is this country thinking of opening any new sea routes or sending out research fleets?"

... They'll be willing to tell me anything.

"No, you absolutely can't do that!" The Japanese tax consultant was blowing up at Mitsuha. "All overseas packages must go through customs inspection! You also have to submit an export declaration to customs for any mail that exceeds 200,000 yen in value. If you don't want to deal with customs yourself, hire a customs broker! It's the only way to obtain an export license. You'll need it to receive reductions on tariffs and consumption tax. You'll get in trouble for smuggling if you don't have one. Normally, you wouldn't be able to get the package on a ship without going through the proper procedure and receiving the necessary documents. Asking a sailor or pilot friend to deliver it for you is a *serious* crime! They could get fired!"

Mitsuha knew there was trouble as soon as the tax consultant told her she needed official documents for overseas shipping. She couldn't tell him about her world-jumping ability, but when she lied and said she was going to ask a friend to deliver the packages for her, he blew his top.

"Don't tell me you already did it." He was so furious that he was quivering. Mitsuha shook her head vigorously.

Holy crap, I could've gotten in serious trouble...

The art she brought to her gallery café last time wouldn't be an issue. She jumped that straight from the other world into that country, so it was never in Japan. That couldn't be considered smuggling. All she had to do to avoid trouble was not send the money from those sales to Japan. She should delete the emails for the orders too.

And her entire browser history while she was at it…

You're wondering about the import procedure for the other country? Ahaha… Well, I'm exempt from taxes over there, so I don't have to worry about tax evasion, at least. I don't know what other tariff laws I'm breaking, though.

Mitsuha chuckled to herself nervously.

I'm not gonna sweat the small stuff!

That's not small stuff?

Yeah… I'm sorry.

It was time to form a strategy. Mitsuha learned a lot at the navy faction party, and she needed to start putting her knowledge to use. She had yet to take any real action because her only goal up until this point had been to gather information, but she couldn't go much longer being passive.

Her top priority was securing the safety of her Yamano County citizens and herself. Her second priority was the safety of the Bozeses, her acquaintances in Zegleus, and those she met on the diplomatic mission. Her third priority was the safety of everyone she'd met in the New World.

Yep, my friends in the New World mean more to me than people I've never met in the Old World. Unfortunately, part of Vanel's modus operandi is finding new lands and exploiting them. If they discover the Old World and invade it, my top three priorities will come into conflict with each other.

Hmm… My only choice might be to act behind the scenes.

It was highly unlikely there were any politicians who'd want to form an equal treaty with a less advanced country when they could easily conquer and exploit them. Nobody who's in power right now, at least. Even if such a benevolent politician existed, they'd be lambasted and chased out of office by other politicians, nobles, merchants, and the citizenry. Any efforts to support such a politician would be a waste of time.

In the end, Mitsuha had no choice but to warn the Vanelians that if they mess with the Old World, they'll regret it. Which meant war was unavoidable. That being the case, her goal should be to prevent as many casualties as she could on both sides and make sure the loser didn't suffer too greatly.

In other words, I need to help our kingdom win.

Even if Zegleus were to win, they weren't capable of crossing the ocean and invading the New World. The war would end when the intruders scrambled back home. At worst, Zegleus would demand reparations and ransoms for prisoners of war.

If Zegleus lost, Vanel would steal all its wealth, capture the people as slaves, and exploit it as a vassal state forever. Mitsuha couldn't let that happen. But one girl couldn't possibly hope to stop a war. Not even the king of Zegleus or Vanel could do that. Naval warfare was inevitable.

I wonder if single-line bombardment from ships-of-the-line-class galleons will be the main tactic by the time the war starts? Or will Vanel even achieve that technology by then...?

There was one major positive to naval warfare: it didn't endanger civilians. Soldiers knew the risk of dying in battle when they chose their occupation. They could hardly complain about being placed in mortal danger when it was their job to travel far from home to kill others.

What about sailors who were forcefully enlisted? That's their fault for going to battle without trying to escape first! The only people who show mercy on the battlefield are those who already have the upper hand and idiots.

Anyway, Mitsuha's next course of action was to extract information from the powerful nobles she met at the parties. She needed to determine who would lean toward peace if Vanel suffered defeat in naval warfare, and search for hints to help her curry favor with those people. Her targets were the high-ranking nobles belonging to navy factions. Military officers who weren't nobles lacked political influence even if they were decently high in rank, so they were less of a priority.

Sweet, the first phase—establishing a base behind enemy lines—is complete! And now with a new objective in mind, gathering more information!

"Very interesting..."

The king of Vanel had summoned a marquis and a count to his palace separately that day. He'd instructed them each to bring their pendant and necklace for an appraisal. The results were shocking.

"To think these are both as valuable as a national treasure, if not more so..." the king murmured. The very best appraisers in Vanel had all given the jewelry the same evaluation. He had no choice but to accept the verdict.

He couldn't ask to keep the jewelry. The accessories were from a foreign noble—a child, no less—gifted as a token of friendship; even a king couldn't get away with such an act. Confiscating them would ruin the king's popularity. He had them appraised and returned to their owners.

"What do you think?" The king turned to his chancellor.

"It is unclear if the jewelry was produced in the girl's country or if she bought them abroad, but that changes little," the chancellor answered.

The king nodded. "The girl has multiple gems worthy of being a national treasure, and she's willing to give them away to people she just met. That begs the question—just how many gems do her *parents* have?

"Do whatever you can to determine what country she hails from. Do *not* harm her; make sure she is treated kindly. Post lookouts around the building she is renting and follow any unidentifiable visitors who come to her. Have multiple people tail her when she goes out. She is bound to meet with a contact from her home country.

"Also, send as many eyes and ears as you can into any party she attends. Have them listen for any slips of the tongue. She may accidentally speak her native language. If we can just figure out where she came from, the rest will be easy. Whether we establish trade with her homeland, apply political pressure, or use military force— regardless of the method, we're sure to obtain vast wealth. I'd rather end this peacefully, though…"

"Do you realize how many days it's been?!" the king of Vanel raged. "Why have you not given me a report yet?!"

"B-Because I have yet to receive any information worth reporting…" the chancellor quavered. "The only customers to enter her shop were Vanelian citizens, and none of them had anything to hide. She had no other visitors and has only left the building to go shopping or visit noble estates. The only other place she's gone to is the bank… And she tends to stay inside for days at a time when she closes the shop."

"Have you gathered nothing at the parties?!"

"I'm afraid those efforts have proven fruitless as well, Your Majesty. She does not fall for leading questions, and we do not recognize any of the words from her native language or names of places we coaxed out of her, such as 'kana-gara' or 'tele-vishun.'

"There are countries where multiple languages are spoken de-pending on the region, and some languages are only used among clergymen or royals. As such, there are languages we don't recognize even within countries we have diplomatic relationships with…"

They were getting nowhere. Running out of patience, the king gave the chancellor an order.

"Get Count Wondred and Viscount Ephred onto the invite list for the next party she attends! I don't care what faction the party belongs to!"

"Huh? But Your Majesty…" The chancellor's eyes widened.

"Just do as I say!"

"Y-Yes, Your Majesty…" He was left with no choice but to com-ply.

Count Wondred and Viscount Ephred were two of the many peerages held by the royal family. They used these whenever they wanted to go to a function that was improper for royals to attend or if they simply wanted to attend as ordinary nobles.

Of course, the entire nobility knew about this, and the royals weren't in disguise or anything. Every Vanelian noble was aware of all the peerages in the kingdom, and they all knew what the royals looked like, so there was no way they could pretend to be someone else. It was an implicit rule that when the royals used the peerages, they were to be treated as if they actually were a count and a vis-count… That said, it was common sense not to be rude and belittle them because of their ranks.

The title of Count Wondred belonged to the king, and the title of Viscount Ephred belonged to the crown prince.

Mitsuha was going to a party. It had only been a week since the last one, but she had nothing to do in this country beyond gathering information and tending to her commodity shop. She finally opened Yamano Commodities a few days ago and had been getting a decent number of customers.

Unsurprisingly, some of the visitors were nobles who wanted to speak to her and scout for hints about her identity, but most of them were of low rank. Most nobles didn't go shopping themselves; instead, they had the store come to their estate with a selection of their top-quality goods. Food and consumables were bought at stores, but rather than go into the city themselves, nobles had people who did the shopping for them. It was apparently too damaging to a noble's pride to trek to the city for shopping errands.

The nobles who visited Mitsuha's shop were proactive and didn't care quite so much about their image. While a few were counts, most of them were of lower rank. Mitsuha spoke about many things with those nobles and gave them little gifts from Japan that were novel but not out of place in this world. Those items weren't for sale; she wanted them to be special rewards for nobles who went through the trouble of coming over regardless of what others might think.

Mitsuha didn't give any gifts to vassals who were sent to scout the shop on behalf of their lords. The vassals looked at her with confusion when they saw her give gifts to nobles and not to them, but she didn't care. She wasn't going to reward a noble who dispatched a lackey on their behalf.

Anyway, the shelves were stocked with a handpicked variety of jewelry, alcohol, silk goods, confectionaries, and other products that wouldn't help improve Vanel's technology or productivity. The lazy shop with irregular hours was up and running. Mitsuha didn't let anyone buy items in bulk to stock up or resell them. She wasn't out to sell goods in large quantities and make bank. This was more like a pop-up shop to promote goods from her homeland.

Wait, that's not why I founded this shop! This place is a front so nobody will be suspicious as to why a young female noble from a faraway land isn't staying at a luxurious hotel!

But you get the idea. I opened the shop, but I'll leave it closed most of the time. And it's closed today because I'm attending my first party in a week. The event isn't until evening, but a proper lady must take her time to get ready. Tending the shop today just wouldn't be feasible.

Mitsuha arrived at the party. The host was a count belonging to an army faction. She would've preferred a navy-faction party, but it would harm Marquis Mitchell's position if she avoided army-faction parties entirely. The marquis was at the party too.

The army couldn't travel to the Old World without the help of the navy. And the Old World was a great distance away for ships in this world; they wouldn't be able to board that many soldiers. A small number of foot soldiers wielding swords, lances, bows, and a few muskets isolated far from home weren't going to be much of a threat. That was why Mitsuha didn't have much interest in the army.

But it wasn't just the navy factions that had influence in the government. It wouldn't be a bad idea to grow friendly with nobles from army factions too, and she wanted to do Marquis Mitchell a favor.

There's just one problem. I've been attending a lot of parties recently. I can't let myself drink alcohol—getting drunk while alone in enemy territory would be an awful idea—but I have to do something as I talk to people, so I've been drinking juice and eating a heck of a lot of food.

I can't fasten my skirts anymore... And my dresses are feeling tight around my belly... This is bad. Really bad!

And why's it only my stomach that's gotten bigger?! Why can't some of that fat go to my chest?! Argh! Damn it, damn it, damn it!

Mitsuha had to take a moment to cool down.

U-Uh, moving on. There are a bunch of army-faction nobles here, which makes it Marquis Mitchell's home turf. I need to turn up the charm and make him look good.

Huh? What's with that group over there? Mitsuha thought as a bunch of people entered the hall.

The parties in Vanel followed a similar style to the ones in Zegleus. The so-called American style where the party began as soon as the first guests arrived and the drinks were served. They weren't like Japanese parties where you had to wait for everyone to arrive and share a toast. Plenty of guests were a little late for that reason. Even so, this particular group stood out.

Normally the heads of noble houses entered parties alone or were accompanied by their wife or son at most. This group, however, consisted of a middle-aged noble, his sixteen- or seventeen-year-old son, and five men who looked like knights. Those five men were quite young; there was a chance they were nobles too, but if they were, their peerage would be quite low, making this party above their station.

Well, I'm a viscount so I don't have the highest rank either, but I'm a different case!

Even stranger was the fact that the knight-like men were all wearing their swords. There were already guards stationed in other rooms and outside the estate, and the guests' personal guards were being served food and non-alcoholic drinks away from the main hall. Nobles had no need to wear a sword at a function. Swords would be a hindrance at a cramped venue, and carrying a weapon was a rude show of distrust towards the host.

Mitsuha could only think of one explanation for why these two nobles brought armed guards. *They're wannabe hoodlums! Acting all big and tough when they have nothing to show for.*

The other guests tried to act naturally around them, but it was obvious they were conscious of the group's presence. They kept a slight distance, which the tough guys probably mistakenly interpreted as fear, puffing up their egos even further.

There's only one way to deal with people like this... Avoid and ignore. If they approach, run. It's better to be safe than sorry. Not that I think they're actually any danger to me.

Oh crap, they're coming! To the food corner! Mitsuha fled toward the buffet.

One of the fundamental rules of etiquette in this country was that you couldn't talk to someone who was holding a plate of food. That should save her from the hoodlums. If they were impudent enough to approach her anyway, she could just act offended and storm off. It was considered especially disrespectful if a man did that to a woman, which was interpreted as treating her as a common peasant. Upending her drink over his head was even deemed acceptable for such an act.

Just as I thought, they won't follow me over here. Sheesh, what a pain...

Mitsuha waited a little while before putting down her plate and talking to other guests, but the two hoodlums hurried toward her as soon as she did. She reacted quickly by fleeing back to the food corner. They repeated this process multiple times, as if they were playing some kind of bizarre game.

Am I in danger? Are these socially-tone-deaf idiots after me in hopes of striking it rich with my home country? Why aren't the host and Marquis Mitchell doing anything to stop them? It's plain as day I'm trying to avoid these guys, but no one is stepping up to protect me. Are they so intent on not getting involved that they don't care about a girl's safety?!

I can't trust anyone here! I'm aborting talks with the count who proposed a deal for jewels earlier! Before Mitsuha could realize, the hoodlums had cornered her. She tried to dash to the food table, but their armed entourage blocked her escape.

The younger noble, who was likely the son of the older man, approached.

"Hello, Lady Mitsuha. Too bad you don't have much of a chest!" he joked loudly.

Every guest in the hall gasped in unison. That included Mitsuha, of course. What he said wasn't just rude. It was downright vicious.

"Wh-Wh-What?!" Mitsuha stuttered at the hoodlum boy's greeting.

I mean, I guess he's a little old to call a "boy." He looks around seventeen. But what made him think he could say that out of nowhere in front of all these people?!

The hall was dead silent. Obviously.

Is this asshole lookin' for a fight?!

If looks could kill, Mitsuha's glare would've had the young man lying in a pool of his own blood. He began to fidget.

"Huh? I, uh, heard that if I consoled you in that manner, you would give me a priceless gem and become my friend…"

Where the hell did you hear bullshit advice like that?! Did you think you were teasing me?! Were you trying to be funny?! That was a straight up insult! Screw off!

…Wait a second. Maybe I can use this offense as an excuse to leave the party. No one would blame me for going home after what he just did. The host wouldn't be at fault, except for the fact that he invited this guest.

Yep, that works!

"…This is an inexcusable slight. I'm going home!" Mitsuha pivoted to leave. The people around her did their best to detain her.

"W-W-Wait! Please don't go!"

"Viscountess Yamano! Please pardon his insolence!"

The other guests desperately tried to bargain.

"I'll teach you my family's secret massaging technique for breast enlargement!"

Oh, can it! If those things worked, my boobs would be bigger by now. You think I haven't tried them all?! Massages, exercises, diets, dubious medicine I bought online, praying to God, you name it! And none of it's done a damn thing!

Huh? Why is it quiet again?

"Viscountess Yamano..." Marquis Mitchell gulped. Why was he looking at her with such pitying eyes? "You said all of that out loud..."

Oh. Great.

Mitsuha screamed at the top of her lungs.

I'm leaving! I don't care what anyone says, I'm gone!

No one tried to stop her as she left the hall.

I'm that pitiful, huh?!

"Wh-What should we do, Father..."

"This is your mess, son. You have to clean it up."

"I figured..."

The two perplexed hoodlums, who were actually Count Wondred and Viscount Ephred—or rather, the king and the prince—stood rooted in place after Mitsuha left the hall. The other attendees looked on in silence, just as perplexed.

"...Sorry," the king—actually, he was Count Wondred at the moment—apologized to the party host. It wasn't a great look for the king to bow to a noble in apology, but this was entirely his son's fault, and he was using his count peerage, so rank wasn't an issue.

"My foolish son robbed you of a chance to form a connection with that girl. An 'acquaintance' of mine will make this up to you. I ask for your forgiveness."

The "acquaintance" he was referring to was himself as the king, obviously. To the host of the party, that promise was payment enough to make up for losing the chance to form a relationship with the foreign girl. He did nothing to offend the girl personally. Technically, storming out of a party for something the host wasn't at fault for was a discourteous act. He could expect an apology and a concession the next time he saw her. This didn't work out so badly for him.

Besides, no one would be callous enough to blame the girl for leaving after what just happened.

Now that their mission had ended in terrible failure, Count Wondred and Viscount Ephred left with their guards as the other guests resumed the party. Unsurprisingly, the event that just transpired dominated conversation.

What in the world would lead a person to make such a misunderstanding?

Could the crown prince be trusted to find a consort on his own? He truly had no understanding of women. Nobles throughout the hall began to scheme about talking their daughters into seducing the naive prince.

As such, the nobles dutifully networked late into the night.

"What the hell is wrong with that guy..." Mitsuha grumbled.

It took a special kind of anger to make it look like steam could be rising from your face. That was how offended Mitsuha was as she stepped in the chartered carriage to return to her shop.

She was going to jump right to her home in Japan once she reached the store, but it was important to keep up appearances, even if it felt like a waste of time and money. There was no way she was going to buy a horse and carriage for herself in this land.

"I can't believe no one stepped up to protect a frail little girl like me from those ruffians... I've had it with army-faction parties!"

Mitsuha was furious.

"Oh, I can use this as a reason not to attend army-faction parties for at least a month. That'll reduce the parties I have to go to and thus, help me trim my waistline! That'll slim me down for sure!"

"What? You're refraining from going to army-faction parties for a while? Why?" Marquis Mitchell exclaimed.

"Because no one did anything to help me even though I *know* everyone realized those weird men were following me around! It'll be navy-faction parties only for me for the next month! Oh, but that doesn't mean I'm gonna attend more navy-faction parties. I'm just removing the army-faction parties from my schedule. Also, tell me the names of the nobles who harassed me!"

"Uh, uhm..."

Marquis Mitchell wanted to explain the situation to Mitsuha, but the king ordered him not to reveal their true identities because he wanted to approach her as an ordinary noble. The other attendees at the party had received the same orders, so they were powerless to help her as well.

But the marquis had to give her something. Disclosing their noble titles shouldn't be an issue; the king was surely going to introduce himself next time he saw her anyway.

"Their names are Count Wondred and Viscount Ephred," he finally confessed.

Mitsuha was puzzled. "I thought they were father and son..."

"W-Well, they are. Their family simply holds multiple peerages, and the oldest son uses the second peerage until he inherits his father's... Just like you, I assume."

"Ahaha..."

Mitsuha was actually the head of her family, but telling people that would only invite unnecessary confusion, so she laughed his comment off. Evading the topic with a vague laugh was a hallmark skill of the Japanese.

So she won't be attending army-faction parties for a whole month... Not ideal, but I don't think I can talk her out of it. That was a cruel thing to say to a young girl in front of so many people. Girls her age are sensitive. Her feelings must've been hurt. What in the world was the prince thinking... Marquis Mitchell worried.

As a member of an army faction, he wasn't thrilled about her decision. But most of his faction was present at the party; they'd understand. If anyone were to complain, it'd seem like they were shaming the prince for his blunder. That would put even more pressure on the traumatized girl. He didn't want to think about what that would lead to. It was hard to imagine anyone taking such a risk.

One month will pass in no time. I've been sending her to a few too many parties recently, anyway. She's starting to put on a little weight— no, she may be a child, but it's rude to think such things about a lady.

Marquis Mitchell's eyes drifted unconsciously to Mitsuha's belly. Mitsuha noticed that, of course.

"Ah..." she gasped.

"Ah?"

"AAAAAAHHHHHHHH!"

"What? Viscountess Yamano isn't coming?"

"Yes, she's feeling under the weather today, apparently..."

Ten days later, Count Wondred and Viscount Ephred attended a navy-faction party that Viscountess Yamano was expected to attend. When they couldn't find her, the king had his subordinate check what was going on, and that was the answer he got.

"Oh well…" the king sighed. "We all get sick sometimes. She's living by herself far from home and isn't used to the food and water of this land. Who could blame her for falling ill. Since we're already here, we may as well speak to some people. It's nice to do so every now and then as Count Wondred, a simple noble of this kingdom. Tell Marquis Mitchell to look after Viscountess Yamano so she doesn't contract any serious illness."

"Yes, Your Majesty!"

The king—or Count Wondred at this moment—was free to attend any party regardless of faction. He just had to wait for the next opportunity to see her.

"Huh? The viscountess isn't here today either?"

"Yes, Your Majesty. She's having one of those days, I heard…"

"A-Ah, I see. She may be a child, but she is still a girl. That's understandable…"

At least she wasn't sick. That meant she should be fine in a matter of days. The king could stomach meeting her a few days later than expected.

"What? She's not here today either?"

"She's absent again? Why?!"

The king was starting to get suspicious. Viscountess Yamano wasn't passing on every party. If she was, her excuse of being sick wouldn't check out. But she seemed to be appearing at all the parties that he and the crown prince refrained from attending out of political consideration.

It's happened too many times to be a coincidence. The nobles noticed it some time ago, and now the king was catching on too.

"She's avoiding us…"

Every time Mitsuha received a party invitation, she first asked Marquis Mitchell if she should attend or not, and if he said yes, she would write an apologetic letter to the host saying that she hadn't been feeling well lately and might have to back out at the last minute. She'd then send a messenger on the day of the party to ask—not the host—but the party's clerk if Count Wondred and Viscount Ephred were on the attendee list. Depending on the answer, she would attend the party as planned or inform the host she couldn't make it.

Word spread throughout the nobility once this happened enough times, and people figured out what caused her to skip parties—the attendance of Count Wondred and Viscount Ephred.

It was normally a massive honor for a noble to have the king and crown prince at their party as discreet guests. That hadn't been the case lately, however. It was clear that the goal behind this rush of party infiltrations was to speak to Viscountess Yamano while pretending to be ordinary nobles, and that they had no interest in mingling with the host. The king and the prince didn't speak to anyone, and as soon as they realized that the viscountess was absent, they left. No host could brag about receiving such a visit from the king. Besides, it was only "Count Wondred" who was attending the party anyway.

Ask any noble if they would want Count Wondred to attend their party at the cost of losing Viscountess Yamano, and they would respond with an emphatic no.

"Why is this happening…" the king mumbled the question he already knew the answer to. It was because of his dumb idea of pretending to be an ordinary noble, and because his son made a daft misunderstanding and insulted the girl.

"WHY IS THIS HAPPENING?!"

Bonus Chapter:
Business Booms at Gold Coin ~Rudina and Sylua~

"Finally, tomorrow is the opening day... Are you ready, Sylua?" Rudina asked.

Sylua nodded.

"I understand it may be hard to have a boss who is four years younger than you—and it's not like I have more experience here than you since we both started on the same day—but you'll have to put up with it. We both have jobs to do. I plan to treat you as an equal at work unless I need to give you an order as the manager."

Sylua sternly nodded again. "Rank and post are all that matter when it comes to pecking order in a workplace. We have a mission to accomplish. Age is irrelevant. You're my superior, Rudina. I will follow your orders."

"Oh... That's good to hear!"

It seemed like Sylua wasn't the annoying type to insist that "younger coworkers should respect their elders!" even if they had a lower position than her. That was a relief. Rudina had already gotten that sense over the last few days as they prepared for opening. She only brought it up for the sake of formality.

Rudina was an underage girl from an orphanage. Sylua was a

seventeen-year-old girl who also seemed to lack any family. There weren't many decent jobs in this country for young girls and children who didn't have relatives, education, money, or connections. A few jobs existed, but they were the kind that was only available to young, attractive girls.

It was a miracle that Rudina found this job. Hell would freeze over before she gave it up. She sensed that Sylua felt the same way.

"I want the menu to consist of dishes that can be made quickly with pre-cooked ingredients. Our food won't be as good as first-class restaurants, but we'll compete on volume, price, and with the taste of old-fashioned home cooking," Rudina said.

While "home cooking" had a nice ring to it, all it really meant was amateur cooking. While "consommé simmered for a week" wasn't something they could offer, a "quick-stewed meal that reminds you of home" could be their strength. They'd use cheap ingredients and offer large portions. That was how this café would compete.

It didn't occur to either of the girls that this menu was more fit for a cheap food court than a café. Neither of them knew what a café was, as their lives had never given them a chance to experience such a place.

"Anyway, we're going to keep that promise we made that day. Are you with me?" Rudina asked. Sylua nodded silently.

The owner is inarguably a good-natured person who is naive about the world. I won't tolerate any betrayal of her kindness.

Crush our enemies and make the owner happy.

They were willing to give their all for the slightly airheaded girl who saved them from rock bottom. Rudina doubted the boss had any intention of "saving" them when she hired the girls—she was just looking for employees—but that didn't matter. This was her first home since she left the orphanage. It was her sanctuary, a castle she needed to protect. She was willing to crush anyone, be it a god or a devil, who tried to take it from her. And if she died doing so, it wouldn't be without taking her enemies down with her.

If Rudina died protecting this café, the owner might give another orphan a chance to work here. That meant another child would receive hope and carry on Rudina's mission. If she could die believing so, it would be a worthy end. How many people in this world had the privilege of dying while knowing that their life had meaning? The thought filled her with contentment.

"I don't plan on dying so easily, though…" Rudina muttered after a short pause. Sylua quietly nodded. She might've been thinking the same thing behind her unexpressive mask. Her reaction couldn't have come so naturally otherwise.

"All right, our battle starts tomorrow!"

"Okay!"

Opening day arrived. Shift one: morning to early afternoon. The café saw zero customers.

Rudina had expected this. They didn't do any prior advertising, so no one knew the café was even open. It was also unlikely anyone would try a new restaurant during their hectic morning commute or lunch break. People tended to choose familiar restaurants during those windows rather than take the time to venture out for a new eatery.

Shopping around for a new dining spot was something you did when you had the time to spare. Dinnertime was just that. It was too soon to worry.

The café fared better during shift two in the evening as occasional customers wandered in to check out the new restaurant. They were stunned when they saw that the chef was thirteen years old, and that the waitress wasn't much older. At first, they were dumbfounded by how filling the dishes on the menu were, but quickly grinned when they saw the cheap prices. The massive portions then floored them all over again.

The waitress was stoic and quiet, but she wasn't unfriendly. It just seemed like she wasn't used to interacting with people, and her sincerity and good looks won customers over. The young chef was always smiling, but it seemed like she was forcing herself to.

The meals were nothing exceptional, but they were somehow comforting. They were your standard stewed dishes that can be found at any restaurant. The only difference was that you got a huge portion for cheap.

As the customers indulged in their enormous meals, their eyes followed the café's waitress. A man swung his arms out in a grand gesture as he was talking to a friend. The waitress passed by at that exact moment holding a tray with a water pitcher and some glasses.

Oh no, he's gonna hit her!

The waitress dodged nimbly.

Huh…

Oh no, that customer knocked a plate off the table with his elbow!

The waitress caught it before it hit the floor.

A customer scooted his chair back suddenly and bumped into the waitress.

Oh no, a plateful of food went flying off her serving tray!

She dashed forward and caught the plate…

…And all the food landed perfectly on the plate?! HOW?!

The waitress wasn't very expressive, but occasionally, she'd let hints of alarm or fluster show on her face—even a faint smile every now and then. The changes in her expressions were minute and easy to miss if you weren't paying attention, only manifesting in the form of a slight curl of a corner of her mouth or a twitch of an eyebrow. But an aficionado would notice and enjoy the subtlety of her emotional range.

I'll never get tired of watching her... The customers sighed in bliss.

The café's customer base steadily grew over time. They referred the new place to their coworkers and friends and brought them along. The cheap prices and the serving speed also won over customers looking for a quick place to eat breakfast or lunch.

Rudina was able to keep the prices so low because there were only two employees to pay, and the owner didn't care about profit or building internal reserves. She could get away with lowering the profit margins. Besides, the ingredients she used weren't expensive.

Making delicious meals using cheap ingredients and selling them for low prices—other restaurants that needed to make a sizable profit couldn't imitate such a business model. Who'd want to manage a restaurant that didn't produce any gains for the owner?

And then there were the "fans." Many of the customers became "Sylua's Expression Analyzers," and others came to play a game of "throw a balled-up napkin at her when she isn't looking." The latter group had a strict rule of only being allowed to throw one ball per meal. No one had succeeded in hitting her yet; Sylua caught every single ball.

Various other bizarre groups started to form, including one that called itself the "Rudina's Forced-Smile Lookout Squad," increasing the café's clientele even more. Gold Coin was already turning a profit.

"Hey! Lady! There's a goddamn bug in my food! Come over here and do somethin' 'bout it!"

It was a few days after the café opened. A thuggish customer was yelling, using the oldest trick in the book to threaten the girls. The other customers looked on worriedly as he thrust the plate in Sylua's face. She studied the bug closely.

"Fried rice topped with a cockroach is 50 cents more than ordinary fried rice. I'm adding the extra cost to your bill."

"Whaaaat?!" cried the thug and every other customer in the café.

"I don't see any seasoning on the cockroach or any sign that it was cooked. It's also fully intact; you'd think it would lose a leg or two after being tossed around in a pan full of rice. You've also eaten all of the rice, leaving the plate empty aside from the cockroach... You should've noticed it sooner. Did you keep eating after you discovered it? If you brought it yourself and added it as a topping, I'm going to have to charge you for that," Sylua explained without batting an eye.

"Wh-Wha..." The thug was speechless at her left-field reaction.

The other customers knew the young man was making false accusations, but they kept quiet and observed in silence. This neighborhood was part of a criminal syndicate's turf. They were called the Rousas Clan. A thug from another turf wouldn't dare try such a stunt here. That meant this scoundrel was almost certainly a Rousas member, and involving yourself with him would only lead to trouble.

"A-Are you off in the head, bitch?! Call the manager! I wanna speak to 'em right now!"

"You called for me?" It was none other than Rudina who stepped out of the kitchen and headed for the counter.

"HUUUUUUH?!" Everyone in the room gaped.

The customers had accepted that the chef was a child. The food

was quite good, so there was no reason to complain. But no one suspected for a second that the little girl was also the manager.

"Wha... Y-You're the manager?!"

"That's right," she replied curtly. There was no reason to share unnecessary information with an enemy. Not even her name was worth giving away.

The thug seemed momentarily thrown off by the revelation, but then he got up and edged in on Rudina across the counter.

"So ya really think it's acceptable to serve shit like this to your customers?" He shoved his plate under Rudina's nose.

After studying it carefully, she retorted, "I'm adding 50 cents to your bill for bringing your own topping." She must've been listening to the conversation earlier.

"How dare you!" The thug pounded both fists on the counter. He leaned over with his left hand on the tabletop and grabbed Rudina by the collar with his right. "Who do you think I am?! I'm with the Rousas—"

"Shut up!" someone screamed, followed by a loud *thunk* sound.

"Whuh…"

The thug froze, his eyes widened. His gaze inched away from the manager and toward his left hand on the countertop. A fork. The prongs had pierced his skin and pinned his hand down.

Sylua was grinding the fork down deeper and deeper as hard as she could.

"GAAAAAAAH!" he screamed, unable to take the pain. He let go of Rudina's collar to punch Sylua in the face, but she swiftly caught his fist and put him in an armlock from behind.

His joint made a cracking sound.

"ARRRGGGHHH!"

If he put any more strength into his arm, he knew it'd break.

Joint fractures, unlike single-bone fractures, didn't heal easily and often left prolonged aftereffects. He couldn't afford to move.

The thug couldn't do a thing but sweat and scream. Sylua gave him a glance and turned to Rudina. "Call the police," she said.

The young manager picked up the phone on the counter by the entrance and called the police. They were on speed dial, so she only needed to press one button. The owner had registered the number herself. It wasn't the public emergency line, but instead the number to the nearest police station. The owner was aware that you're supposed to call the emergency number, but she instructed them to use the registered number in an emergency anyway. Rudina did exactly as ordered.

It only took one ring before someone picked it up.

"This is the gallery café, Gold Coin. There's a robber in the restaurant." Calling the thug a robber was fair; there wasn't much difference between brandishing a weapon and grabbing a little girl by the collar.

"**Move out, now! There's a robber at the café!**" hollered the man on the other end of the line. He didn't even wait for her to explain.

Not a second later, the sound of the disconnect tone was all Rudina could hear.

"He hung up…" She was left dazed, receiver still in hand.

Bam!

"Put your hands in the air!"

The door busted open and armed police officers flooded into the café.

"That was way too fast…" breathed the little store manager.

The police station was close; the owner had prioritized safety when she chose the location, so that was intentional. But there was no way the officers should've gotten there as quickly as they did. They had to have dropped everything and sprinted here as soon as the person on the phone shouted. Distance-wise, it was faster to run from the station to the café than to grab a key, go to the parking lot, and drive a patrol car or a motorcycle. And that's exactly what they did.

It was fortunate that Sylua was the one who was holding down the thug. The police officers were acting like rabid wolves. Had the subduer been a customer that the police didn't recognize, they might've shot them both, no questions asked. That was how erratically they were behaving.

Why did so many of them come, anyway? It looked like the whole department rushed over. They'd also barged in without a second thought, each one in a full-on panic. Wasn't it normal procedure to first inquire if there were any hostages or guns, and then surround the building and call for surrender? Why did they just bolt through the door like that?

It didn't make sense.

Anyway, the police were here. Sylua passed the thug over to the officers and one of them handcuffed him. The thug regained his composure when Sylua let go of him.

"A-Arrest these bitches!" he wailed. "That one assaulted me, a *customer!* I'm a member of the Rousas Clan! The old man ain't gonna like it if you arrest me!"

A look of resignation came over the other customers.

The Rousas Clan was a criminal syndicate that ruled this area. They'd given many bribes to the police. Officers were people just like anyone else, and they didn't want to put their loved ones at risk by trying to bring a member of the clan to justice. The clan didn't target the officers themselves—they came after their family and friends.

All the police had to do was accept the bribes and turn a blind eye to any Rousas Clan activity, and otherwise do their jobs. That was just the way it was.

"The old man" the thug mentioned was the boss of the clan. He wasn't his father; that was just what the gang members called him. Even a young grunt like him was under the syndicate's full protection. The customers knew exactly what would happen if the police arrested him—he'd be acquitted, and Sylua would be taken away by the Rousas Clan.

The victorious grin on the thug's face greatly contrasted the gloom of the customers. His expression was slimy, like he was thinking about what he was going to do to the girl who assaulted him. He stuck his cuffed hands toward the officer who'd just put them on.

"What're you waitin' for?! Take these off!"

The officer grabbed the handcuffs…and yanked the thug closer.

"Enough of your nonsense! You're coming with us, punk!"

"Huh?" The other customers gaped.

That was strange. The officer was actually apprehending a member of the Rousas Clan. They couldn't believe what was happening.

Rudina turned to the officer, concerned. "Don't you have to tell him his rights when you arrest him? I thought the arrest would be invalidated otherwise…"

The officer laughed. "Oh, don't worry about that. Where he's going is much scarier than the police department. We're gonna learn all about his background, his foreign connections, and anything else we should know. He's going someplace where his human rights don't matter."

Can they do that? And is it okay to admit it so openly? Rudina was doubtful. But seeing Sylua nodding without a hint of suspicion, *I guess this is just one of those things,* she concluded.

This was a small country, after all. For better or for worse, you could do pretty much anything as long as you had money and power. Better, of course, meant "better for me."

The police officers took the thug away. Later that day, Rudina and Sylua received compensation for the broken tableware. It was significantly more than they needed, though, and even stranger, its sender was the Rousas Clan. The excessive amount of money was probably meant as an apology, and to signal that they won't retaliate.

"What are we going to do with this money…?" Sylua asked.

"We're going to use it to replace broken tableware, of course," Rudina answered firmly.

"What about the rest of the money?"

"We'll contribute it to our earnings."

"Aha…"

"Haha!"

"Ahahahahaha!"

After some thought, they both decided on how they'd spend the money that had fallen into their laps. Rudina was going to give her entire share to the orphanage. Sylua said she was going to "buy an arm." Did she mean a grabber tool…?

It was a stormy day with heavy rain. The weather normally kept people from going out, which meant it was going to be a slow day for restaurants. Some eateries didn't even bother to open on such days.

However, some businesses didn't believe in closing due to bad weather. The girls at Gold Coin didn't want to disappoint the customers who braved the elements to come out, only to find out it was closed. As long as the restaurant had customers who looked forward to dining with them, they wouldn't close without prior notice.

The newly opened gallery café, Gold Coin, fell into the latter group.

"Why's this place so crowded today?! It's pouring outside!" a diner complained.

Gold Coin was so packed that customers were having to share tables with strangers.

"Why'd you decide to eat here today?" another diner questioned.

"Because of this weather. I figured the poor café would be empty if I didn't come. That would make Sylua and the manager kid sad. I don't want this place to go under, either..."

"I don't think you're the only one who had that thought," smiled the second man. "We all may be more alike than we know..."

Business was booming for Gold Coin. And, weirdly, even more so on rainy days.

Afterword

Hi there. It's FUNA.

Saving 80,000 Gold in Another World for my Retirement has finally reached volume four. We're almost halfway to my goal of making it to double digits. Thank you very much!

In this volume, Mitsuha returned from her trip, strengthened her footing in Japan, and secured a base in another country on Earth. She also finally went to the New World, the home of the invading fleet!

And now, standing in Mitsuha's way is the aggressor nation, the kingdom of Vanel. She also had to overcome another colossal obstacle, the Japanese tax office!

Coming up in volume five, Yamano County goes to war with a country on Earth!

Mitsuha: "I can be quite ruthless, you know?"

Colette: "The name's Colette, and I'm the spirit of the ship *Aeras*..."

Sabine and Colette are kidnapped, more episodes at the bizarre gallery café, and a young girl pursues her ambition in *As the Crow Flies a Roflcopter*.

Mitsuha: "I'm one step closer to my goal…"

Check out the newest chapters on the webcomic magazine, Suiyobi no Sirius (http://seiga.nicovideo.jp/manga/official/w_sirius/), on the second and fourth Fridays of each month!

The anime for my other series *Didn't I Say to Make My Abilities Average in the Next Life?!* begins airing in October!

Also in October is the release of *I Shall Survive Using Potions!* novel series volume five. The whole month is jam-packed with FUNA series! Please look forward to it!

My sincerest thanks to my editor, the illustrator, the binding designer, the proofreaders, the printing, publishing, distribution, and sales staff, the administrators of Shosetsuka ni Naro, the readers who pointed out writing errors and gave me advice in the comments section, and of course, everyone who picked up this book.

Thank you so much!

I hope to see you again in the next volume.

FUNA

FUNA

My dream of becoming an interplanetary spaceship captain dissipated before it even left the atmosphere.

But my dreams of becoming a writer and traveling to another world came true—Mitsuha and the gang made that happen.

On top of it all, with the manga and anime adaptations, this novel took me beyond my wildest dreams.

We've come this far; let's keep going just a little further...to see how far they'll take us!

Illustrator
Touzai
I have no words for I am but a novice.

Self-improvement. That's all there is.

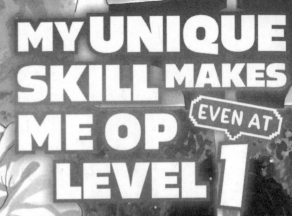